FOR REFERENCE

theblackchord

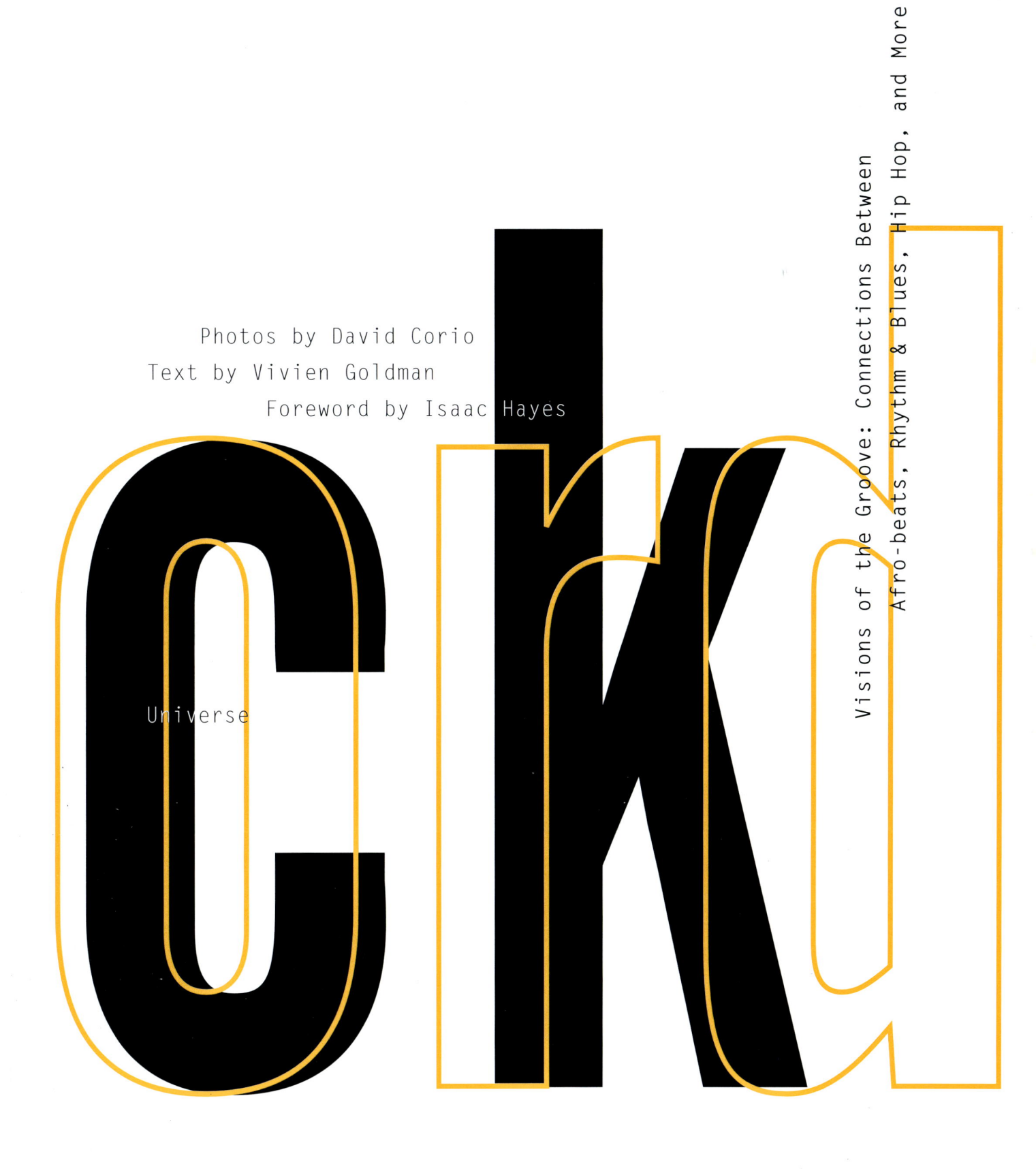

Photos by David Corio
Text by Vivien Goldman
Foreword by Isaac Hayes

Universe

Visions of the Groove: Connections Between Afro-beats, Rhythm & Blues, Hip Hop, and More

Thanks From David Corio:
I would like to thank for their guidance, inspiration, and support; Pat & Cyril Corio, Lai Ngan & Tung Walsh, Suki, Nik, & Lou, Jayne Rockmill, Naomi Warner, Dotun Adebayo, Jon Baker, Steve Barrow, Janette Beckman, Mark Borkowski, Barnie Bubbles, David Calderley, Lyn Champion, Mary Corcoran, Chris Wells and all at Echoes, Flat Iron Lab in NY, Chris Gabrin, everyone at Greensleeves, Malu Halasa & Andy Cox, Chris & Nancy Givens at Heartbeat, Jacqui Juceam, Julie Grahame and all at Retna US and UK, Meg Handler at the Village voice, Chris Krage, Mike Krage, Tiina Loite, Cathy Mather, Noemi Masliah, Tony McDermott, Ian McCann, Matt Snow & Suzie Hudson at Mojo, all past and present NME, Marianne Rohrlich, Jon Pareles, Neil Strauss and Zvi Lowenthal at the New York Times, Michael Ochs Archive, Suzanne Richie, Felice Rosser, S.I.N., Geoff Smyth, Neil Spencer, Helen Heely at the *Times*, V.P. Records and Val Wilmer.

Thanks From Vivien Goldman:
Thanks to my family for everything. Thanks to the Think Tank, particularly Tom Terrell, Jumbo Vanrenen, Dave Hucker, Bill Adler, Eve Parkes, Isaac Fergusson, Larry Birnbaum, Rob Kenner, Chris Salewicz, Teresa Kereakes, Stanley Mieses, Sean Barlow and Banning Eyre at Afropop, Roy Carr, Karen Walter at New Musical Express, John Sutton-Smith, Roger Steffens, C. C. Smith and The Beat, J-C Yebga Likoba and Don Pullen's Africa-Brazil Connection, Lekan Babalola and the Yoruba Jazz People, and those fabulous Fictionaires, Evelyn McDonnell and Jana Martin.

To those who heard the Black Chord and helped: the BBC's Kim Evans and Anthony Wall and Jessica Taylor at 'Arena'; Suzette Newman, Simon Goffe, Eugene Manzi, Brian Jones at Violator, Peter Himberger, Brian Bacchus, Jordan at Nile Rodgers' Productions, Harry Weinger, Michelle Spence, Marie and all at Isaac Hayes' office, and Mr. Derek 'Off The Hook' Kahn All my editors over a quarter century, including: Nick Logan, Alan Lewis, Richard Williams, Neil Spencer, Evelyn McDonnell, Eric Weisbard, Mark Kemp, Eve MacSweeney, Tim White, Deborah Gregory, Dominic "Apeman" Kenny, Caspar Llewellyn-Smith, Ray Rogers, and of course, Miss Universe, Gena Pearson. And respect to Charlie Comer, 1935-1999. Show business was his life.

First published in the United States of America in 1999
by UNIVERSE PUBLISHING
A Division of Rizzoli International Publications, Inc.
300 Park Avenue South
New York, NY 10010

© 1999 Universe Publishing

All rights reserved. No part of this publication may be reproduced, stored in a retrieval system, or transmitted in any form or by any means, electronic, mechanical, photocopying, recording, or otherwise, without prior consent of the publishers.
99 00 01 02 / 10 9 8 7 6 5 4 3 2 1

Printed in Italy

Library of Congress Cataloging-in-Publication Data
Corio, David.
The black chord: visions of the groove: connections between Afo-beats, rhythms & blues, hip-hop, and more / by David Corio and Vivien Goldman; foreword by Isaac Hayes.
p. cm.
ISBN 0-7893-0337-X (hc)
ISBN 0-7893-0357-2 (pb)
1. Afro-Americans--Music--Pictorial works. 2. Popular music--Social apects--United States.
I. Goldman, Vivien II. Title.

r 781.64 C813b 1999
Corio, David.
The black chord : visions of
the groove : connections

**8  INTRODUCTION:** Connections. The foundation of all music springs from Africa, spreading new branches and expressing itself uniquely wherever it stretches. From funk to the sacred, musicians are guardians of traditions deep within our collective memory.

**14  ROOTS AND CULTURE:** Spirituality has always been a serious force in Black music, starting with the tradition of drumming, chanting, and revelations. In African America, churches are a consistent unifying force; gospel's classic voices take to nightclubs and find commercial success. Pop artists smuggle sacred concerns into their infectious grooves. In the jazz world, the spiritual quest informs experimental music. Still close to its holy drums, Rastafarian reggae rallies a global movement. On the dance floor, trance music transports ravers.

**54  HEART AND SOUL:** Perhaps the greatest of all subjects, love songs express urges that transcend nations and generations, from smooth 1950s crooners to today's balladeers. Changes in generations and society are palpable in the contrast between the lascivious double entendres of the blues, the idealized romantic yearning of 1950's doo-woppers, and the explicit lust of hardcore urban artists and Jamaican dancehall's grind queens.

**98  REVOLUTION:** Black music has a history of performers whose art was matched by their commitment even in the face of conflict. Whether facing assassination, torture, or police harassment, these courageous heroes and heroines of Black music fought oppression and injustice in their lives and in their music. Artists of honor tell it like it is.

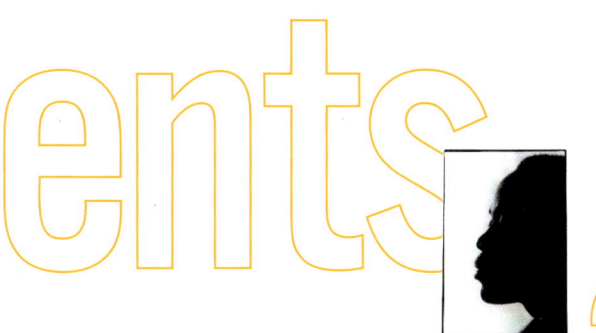

ents

**138  EXPLORERS:** In the Black music continuum, there have always been adventurous spirits who acknowledge barriers only to use them as rites of passage. Such innovators invent new musical languages like scratching or dubbing. Other explorers might project a vision of alternate realities, parallel space universes, that becomes a manifesto, rallying fans into a common cry.

# foreword

BY ISAAC HAYES

As you look through these pages, you'll see the faces of some musicians I know, love, and respect, and others whose work makes me feel like I know them. Some of these folks and their music may be strangers to you, but they're all worth meeting.

There are singers of love songs that demonstrate all the different ways we musicians have of showing our emotions. Life can be a struggle and socially committed artists in this book sing about it, or have even died for it. We're all surrounded by different boundaries that try to limit us, but experimental performers find a way to break through and share their reality with new kinds of music.

The original rhythms of the music we hear on the radio in America and Europe today came up from the Caribbean and Africa. Those are the roots. The grooves took on different vibrations in different locations, and you can still hear them now in hip-hop and R&B.

When I had the opportunity to go to Africa and visit the villages, I heard the real, raw, true rhythms and realized the origins of the music that I was raised on. It reminded me of who I was and where I came from and that I owe it to myself to pursue my history.

We should all take lessons and understand the whole odyssey of music coming from Africa to where it is today, so that we can have a deeper appreciation of how music came to be where it is.

I first heard African drum rhythms and chants at the movies and they weren't too different from the old Negro spirituals I grew up with in the South. There was a relationship. Though I didn't know anything much about Africa, it felt familiar.

During slavery, Black people were only allowed to sing those spirituals and eventually the blues, which evolved into a cry of the people. You worshipped, celebrated religious faiths and beliefs, or you lamented the oppression, via spirituals or gospel. You sang for deliverance or the hereafter; the relief, the celebration of passing over from this life to another.

That spirit resonates a lot in popular music. It sounds more contemporary, but the message is always there.

Oney  Ocho Rios, Jamaica 1986

in

# INTRODUCTION

The ancient stone of "The Door of No Return" frames blue sea on the isle of Goree off the coast of Dakar, Senegal. It was here that some five million enslaved Africans were pushed through this narrow passage and shipped to the unknown Americas. Untold captives flung themselves into the sea rather than face an ominious future. But forces of human renewal are such that from the ashes of despair beauty can arise, and shattered races can—astoundingly—survive.

This grim doorway proved to be a birth canal for the many musics that African descendants continue to forge in America, Britain, the Caribbean, and South America. A musical continuum. The black chord.

"When I look at that door, my mind travels in time," reflected the Senegalese musician Baaba Maal. "I try and imagine how many people passed through there and which facets of our culture they took with them. In Africa, we see music as a tree and Africa is the foundation; music—like blues or rap—is the branches. When I see Michael Jackson dance, I recognize something that comes from very far away. Maybe he feels he created it, but cultural expression sleeps within us through the generations until someone feels it. Because culture is something that can never disappear."

The black chord is a lineage and a vibration that resonates through the meditations of jazz saxophonist Ornette Coleman, through the pulse of reggae lion Bob Marley's anthems, through the forceful caress of Miriam Makeba's voice, or through the sassy, sexy swing of Missy Elliott's rap. The Jamaican dub poet, Michael Smith, mourned, "The oppressed and the dispossessed can't get no rest." Yet with great tenacity, Africans throughout the diaspora have woven the black chord, as an assertion of strength and identity in an often hostile, constricting society.

The African seed of sound was transplanted everywhere, always expressing a unique situation and sensibility. In America, delta blues took the train up north, went electric, and sparked rock'n'roll. Digging hot New Orleans rhythm'n'boogie, Jamaicans rolled their own ska, reggae, and dancehall. The musicians of the French Antilles put the prance of European quadrilles into their zippy zouk. The sacred drums of Brazilian samba are steeped in the yearning of Portuguese folk songs. Multicultural Britons put reggae bass and high-energy synthesized drums into a blender and whirled them up into techno music. Drawing on memories of Africa's oral tradition, African-American rap grew to be the global language of the late twentieth century and inspired young rappers and techno DJs in Africa.

This cross breeding of music is a miracle of survival and creativity. Over centuries the tale does not come full circle. Rather, it is an infinite spiral-dance of exchange and communication that draws inside each new generation.

Coming from the South, the R&B singer Monica was mainly exposed to blues and gospel. "Cable TV gave me the opportunity to explore African culture and its music. The intensity and spirituality they put into it makes me have ultimate respect for them. Behind the way they

Papa Wemba New York 1998

dance and chant is a meaning, and it's time that we pay attention and homage to those things. It's time to bring different types of people and music together."

The black chord is not a straightforward history. Rather, it is an emotive sampling of some of the artists whose music, ideas, and lives are so enriching. This book traces the music that made it across the old trade routes during slavery, when ships plied what was once the Middle Passage between Africa, Britain, the Americas, and the Caribbean. Stops on the way included Brazil, Cuba, France, and South Africa.

In each territory, music became not only enjoyment but also a means of identifying the artists' communities.

Though he was a dictator after colonial rule, Zaire's Mobutu Sese Seko enforced a program in the 1960s called L'Authenticité that fostered local music and dance by staging national competitions. It worked well enough that even when artists fled his regime, they brought with them their new national spirit. The Zairean *soukous* singer Papa Wemba was famous in 1980s Paris as the king of the *sapeurs*—young African fashion plates who rivaled one another in their designer duds and fancy dances.

"The period of President Mobutu's L'Authenticité helped us a lot because we went back to traditional music," reflected Papa Wemba. "Our heads were full of new ideas."[1]

Indeed, the urge for authenticity still links all the music in the black chord. It's what the rap mantra, 'Keepin' It Real,' is all about. Even a music that likes to present itself as uncut hedonism like 1970s disco or 1990s acid house is still a rallying cry—a shout of identity, self-definition, and resistance.

But like everything else, authenticity changes. The world has moved beyond those narrow definitions. The total immersion and reinterpretation of Jamaican reggae by a Ghanaian Scottish singer like Finley Quaye is advance indication of how people will continue to create in ways that express their reality, throughout the new millennium.

Because, as they say in Jamaica, "Who feels it, knows it."

New York 1999

*monica*

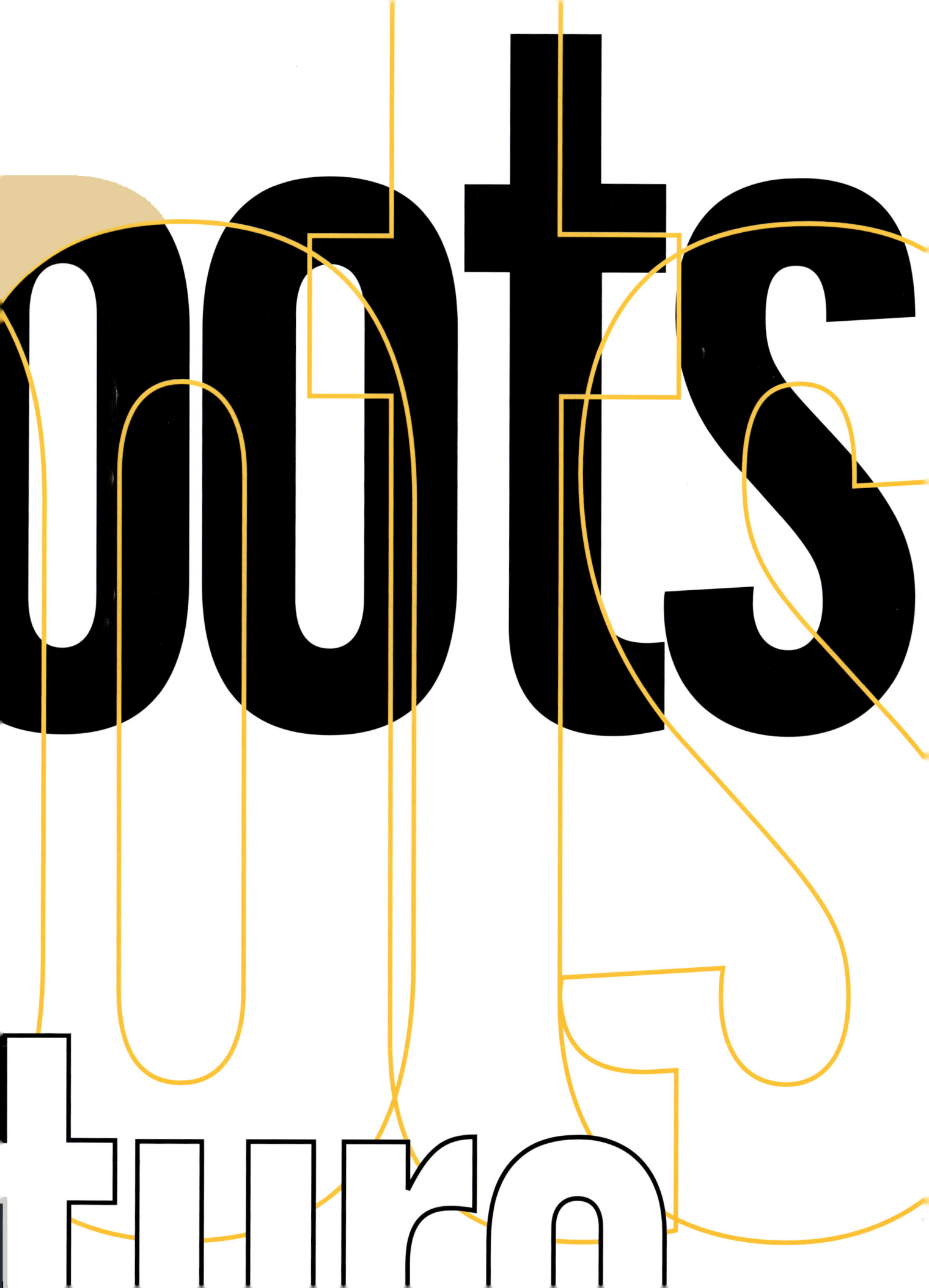

Will Gaines, London 1984

# Roots & Culture

## Culture

Our instruments, ourselves—music's basics are the voice and human percussion, using the body itself as a drum. Witness the organic Pygmy percussion of playing nature—hitting a tree with two sticks or rhythmically slapping water as it rushes over rocks.

People can make an incredible range of sounds, solo. In tap, feet are the drumsticks and the ground is the drum. Tap happened when West African "juba" step dances synchronized with European clog dances. It shone in early twentieth century entertainments like minstrel shows and the Theater Owners Booking Agency's T.O.B.A. (commonly called Tough On Black Asses) a vaudeville circuit that lasted until the Depression. Tappers like Charles "Sandman" Sims, and Honi Coles, and Will Gaines found their match in the unpredictable bebop drumming of the 1940s.

"They are almost like drummers and you can learn a lot just listening to the rhythms they get from their taps,"[2] Miles Davis recalled. "In the daytime, outside Minton's (bebop's 1950s Harlem nightclub home) next to the Cecil Hotel, tap dancers used to come up there and challenge each other on the sidewalk."

Along with other cool 1940s boppers like Slim Gaillard, Gaines split for bohemian London in the 1980s. They both became icons-in-residence, inspiring Britain's acid jazz movement. Their presence encouraged a generation of British jazzers like Courtney Pine to develop their own Caribbean-inflected British jazz using hip-hop technology.

Even when tap went underground there were always dancers still hoofing it in the spolight. Outside of the old-timers, Gregory Hines seemed to become the solitary Mr. Tap. Then a dreadlocked homeboy, Savion Glover put a spring in tap's step in the 1990s. His griot-like musical, *Bring in 'Da Noize, Bring in Da Funk*, was a dramatic tap journey through the history of African America.

Tap dancers talk with their feet. The composer, conductor and spontaneous inventor, Bobby McFerrin, made his whole body and voice the instruments for his hit song "Don't Worry, Be Happy." So blithe, seemingly so simple, "Don't Worry, Be Happy," became a global catchphrase.

In the 1980s Doug E. Fresh put a new twist on going solo—a twist influenced by his Harlem hip-hop background. Like Darren Robinson of the comedic rap group, the Fat Boys, Fresh billed himself as "The Human Beatbox." His bleeps, clicks, and boings were so distinctive that in a neat reversal, an actual beatbox—the Oberheim Emulator synthesizer—installed a Doug E. Fresh sound chip in 1986.

McFerrin and Fresh amaze by playing their bodies in unexpected ways as does LadySmith Black Mambazo. This South African Zulu harmony group's unadorned voices are a smooth rush. Ladysmith's unique sound has been used internationally to advertise a variety of products, from Coca-Cola to "Inkneyzi Nezazi," their ode to Heinz baked beans which became a chart hit in England. Listeners respond to their sound without needing to understand the mystic metaphors of their leader, Joseph Shabalala. The group comes from a rich tribal choral tradition that was partly developed in apartheid South Africa's grim male migrant worker hostels as a way to escape from loneliness and abuse.

In West Africa, the voice was the only instrument needed by griots—the guardians of verbal culture—to deliver their ancestral epics.

Yet many chose to complement their words with a silvery sweep of notes from the twenty-one-stringed *kora* (a harp-lute instrument).

"Telling two hundred years of history takes a long time. Some of our songs last two days. They speak of kings and how they fought for power, and how they tried to make their kingdoms strong,"[3] wrote Foday Musa Susa, a Gambian griot and kora master in his book *Jali Kunda: Griots of West Africa and Beyond*. Research for the book took Susa to the five griot countries of the old Manding empire: Mali, Senegal, Guinea-Bissau, Guinea-Conakry and The Gambia.

In the 1980s, three musicians spearheaded Manding culture's popularity—Mali's Salif Keita and Senegal's Baaba Maal and Youssou N'Dour. In the world of popular music, their sound has become known as "The Griot Groove." Artists like Guinea's Oumou Dioubate and Sekouba Bambino follow in their footsteps. But these pioneers paid a price in going against their families' wishes.

Even though N'Dour's mother was a *griotte*, his father disapproved of his decision to become a singer. Nonetheless, N'Dour has been a star since his keening, compelling voice was broadcast on national radio, singing at the funeral

**Ladysmith Black Mambazo** New York 1993

**Bobby McFerrin** London 1985

"In songs about slavery, we sing about which kings fought each other and who was captured,"[4] he wrote.

Susa bridges old and new worlds. He collaborates with artists as diverse as composer Philip Glass, trumpeter Don Cherry, and pianist Herbie Hancock. He also has absorbed the traditional one-hundred-and-eleven songs in his canon. "I studied in the home of my teacher and uncle Saikou Suso for seven years, studying at night. In exchange, I worked in the fields."[5]

A complicated social etiquette governs the griots. Making music is reserved for their caste and is frowned upon for outsiders. The musicians are respected and needed, yet they have low social status.

of the beloved singer, Pape Samba Diop. N'Dour was twelve years old.

In the first band he formed, Super Etoile de Dakar (Dakar Superstar) N'Dour pioneered singing in his language—Wolof—and made use of the *mbalax* sound with its signature use of the flailing two-headed *sabar* drum. British musician Peter Gabriel and Amnesty International, a human rights group, helped introduce N'Dour globally.

Many griot epics were dedicated to the feats of the Manding emperor and warrior, Sundiata Keita. His descendant, Salif Keita, updated the style on the album, *Soro*. It was produced by Ibrahim Sylla in Paris during the early 1980s. Married with synthesizers Keita's unearthly piercing vibrato gives the machines soul.

Savion Glover New York 1998

Born albino, Salif's pallor was regarded as a curse in Mali. He compounded his rejection by becoming a singer. "Children spat at me as I passed," he recalled. Eventually Salif ran away from home and found fame with the Rail Band of Bamako.

Despite his father's objections, Maal was eager to learn and was adopted into the griot family of blind guitar player, Mansour Seck. After studying at the École des Beaux Arts in Paris, Maal traveled the villages of Mali and Senegal, learning from the old griots.

"Salif Keita, Youssou N'Dour, and I were a generation that grew up with traditional music

Fat Boys London 1985

around us," Maal said. "Now the world has changed. Young people aren't staying in the villages any more. In the city, there's no contact with the ceremonies of the oral tradition; people are too busy trying to eat."

Breaking down old barriers, Maal is enthusiastic that his band members come from different ethnic groups. He paid tribute to the African/Jamaican connection with the dance track, "Yella! It Sounds Like Reggae!" In the same spirit, he has incorporated Irish voices in his music, specifically the Screaming Orphans—Sinead O'Connor's back-up band.

"When I heard Irish music it was something so deep. I know there is a connection in the past." The mesh of their voices recalls the black Moors who once ruled Ireland. It's an ancestry that's been explored by bands from such diverse groups as the British ravers, Afro-Celt Sound System and Wingless Angels—a group consisting of Jamaican Rasta Nyabinghi drummers who were recorded by the Rolling Stones' Keith Richards. The Irish band, Chieftains, in their Celtic-Cuban exploration recall the same ancestry on the album, *Santiago*.

In villages and cities all across Africa, music was not entertainment. Babatunde Olatunji, a Nigerian singer, remembers, "Drumming was going on in my village every day. When someone passed into the spirit world we celebrated with songs and drums and chants, or when a baby was born or a young man or woman went through a rite of passage like getting married." Olatunju reintroduced the sound of pure African drums to America with his *Drums of Passion* series in the 1950s.

Making a drum is a sacred process for the drummers of Burundi. As one explained, "Before we make a drum we go into the forest and find the tree that we feel is right. Then we pray to it and pour liquor on its roots as a libation. This makes the tree understand we have not come in a malicious spirit, but so that it can be used for a sacred purpose."

So powerful is the drum that under slavery, its use was banned in America in 1692. Echoes of this prohibition occured throughout the years. In the tradition of rock and rap, bad boys created the shimmering tremolo lilt of steel pan bands. In Trinidad the steel pan has become a source of enormous cultural pride. The instrument and the culture it represents was silenced when the British colonial administration and the Catholic Church banned traditional drums along with the African-derived Shango religion in the years preceding the Second World War.

The steel pan creators were ghetto roughneck "Bad Johns" living where the police were afraid to go. In defiance of the ban they used a chisel and heat to tune a honeycomb of flattened octagonal sections from the oil barrels of the island's greatest export. "Banging iron," the Bad Johns marched into fierce battles with both the police and rival steel orchestras in Port-of-Spain. Orchestras like the many-time Carnival winners, Exodus, rose from gang entertainment by refining music. They created interpretations of Beethoven, Bach, and local composers Pelham Goddard and Lord Kitchener.

Crucial to ancient African science, the drum stirred listeners into a sacred frenzy that

Doug E Fresh

New York 1995

Baaba Maal
New York 1998

20

# Salif Keita

New York 1998

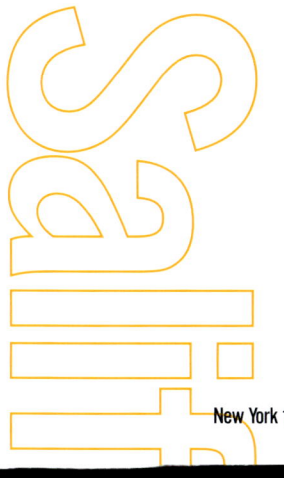

21

connected the everyday and the spirit world, particularly in Cuba and Haiti. Haitian slaves were allowed to make their own *tanbour* (single-headed drums) in the West African style, and though the practice was illegal until 1987, the voodoo forces summoned by the drums were omnipresent.

Though cloaked in Catholicism, these Haitian forces were capricious or benevolent African spirits of the earth, river, and sea much like the Trickster of the Yoruba people in Nigeria. These deities were carried into bondage with Haiti's voodoo and absorbed into Cuba's Santeria, Jamaica's obeah, Trinidad's Shango and Brazil's Candomble. Each spirit had its own color and rhythm that can still be heard in popular as well as ritual music.

Brazil's African heritage is strongest in the coastal town of Salvador, Bahia, from whose hillside squatter camps or favelas the velvet timbre of Virginia Rodriguez attracted the support of Brazil's musical elite. The *tropicalismo* stars of the 1960s—Milton Nascimento, Gilberto Gil, and Caetano Veloso—were among those who mixed electronic rock with traditional rhythms and coded lyrics that criticized the military government. A consistent force in Brazilian music, they united to work with Rodriguez in the 1990s. Rodriguez began singing in the choir of her parents' Protestant church. "I was in another world," she said. "As I matured I wanted to know more about my roots and ancestors. Through *Candomble*, I learned more about my people. To relate to the orixas, in the ceremonies we dance, sing and drum."

Cuba taught America and Europe about rhythm, passion, and seductive tension with its stately sons: the rhumba, the mambo, and the cha-cha-cha. Rhumba became a particular obsession in colonial West Africa where the bandleader and guitarist Franco and his O.K. Jazz, developed the melodious Congo language, "rhumba lingala."

Cuban musician and actor Desi Arnaz used the term *babalawo*, a Santerian bishop, to inject the religion into the heart of American TV culture. Arnaz shouted "Babalu!" in his theme tune for the "I Love Lucy" comedy series. But the love affair between America and Cuba was shattered when Fidel Castro toppled General Juan Batista for government leadership in 1959. Cuba was boycotted culturally as well as politically. Immediately upon Castro's ascent to power, the first wave of Cubans left for New York and Miami.

Cuban trumpeter Jésus Alemany was just a child when these artists left. He grew up within Castro's socialist system. Like all other professional Cuban musicians he was taught and eventually paid by the state for playing gigs in places like Havana's famous Tropicana nightclub, alongside leading Cuban combos like Irakere and Los Van Van. Relocating to London in the 1990s, he gathered key players from home and put together the group Cubanismo! "People think that in the period of isolation there was nothing going on in Cuba, but that is not true. We developed the rap sound *timba*, and brought the African drum, the *bata*, into the popular music a lot more."

The drum is a source of renewal. Some of the greatest jam sessions never recorded must have been those thunderous nights of drumming in seventeenth-century New Orleans' Congo Square. Now Louis Armstrong Square, it is described by the Neville Brothers as "the place where American music was born." Here African slaves of all ethnic groups would transcend their Wolof, Fon, Ashanti, and Yoruba language barriers with their drums. The Neville Brothers call it "that mojo in motion" in their track, "Congo Square." It was a place that attracted audiences of all classes and complexions. They were forging new conjunctions and absorbing the sounds around them—sailors' shanties, Wesleyan hymns, the sprightly quadrille, and jolly brass bands of Europe.

The versatile musician, arranger, and producer Quincy Jones reflected, "Thank God that the Spanish and the French were in New Orleans or we would have really been in trouble because the Protestants would have blown it (the culture of drums and music) away."[6]

Commercialization cannot sift out the sacred from New Orleans music culture. The exuberant bottle-and-can banging and brass bands of the "second line" in a New Orleans funeral procession was an inspiration for trumpeters like the romantic Terence Blanchard and the classicist, Wynton Marsalis.

At Trinidad's Carnival, the same clanking-bash rings throughout the main streets of pre-dawn Port-of-Spain. During Carnival, half-clad revelers splashed in paint and mud prance ecstatically behind the steel bands. In Brazil, too, Carnival is the climax of a lengthy build-up of preparations for Mardi Gras.

In humble dwellings, clapboard shotgun houses, and ramshackle projects, the keepers of Carnival spend months concocting visual delights of feathers, sequins, and beads. Resplendent in this bright regalia, "Indian bands," who parade

and play through the streets, are an essential element of Mardi Gras. They are a spiritual link to Native American traditions.

Flag wavers for the New Orleans sound, the Neville Brothers first joined their Uncle Jolly in the Wild Tchoupitoulas Indian band, in 1976. Indian bands have a lengthy lineage. Big Chief Theodore Emile "Bo" Dollis first "masked" (joined the Carnival "krewes") as a Golden Arrow in 1957 before becoming Big Chief of the Wild Magnolias in 1964. Bands like these have a long history of merrymaking.

The morning after the revelry, Ash Wednesday, the costumes are destroyed, symbolizing the passing of all things like the colored sand of a Buddhist mandala blowing away in the wind.

Awareness of mortality only raises the volume on New Orleans' *laissez les bon temps rouler* (let the good times roll) spirit. It gives music the distinctive, rollicking flourish heard in the dashing piano motifs of the legendary Professor Longhair. Fats Domino was among the many artists who Longhair influenced. The genial piano man was famous for R&B songs like "Blueberry Hill" that expressed the high spirits of early rock'n'roll.

The seeds for musical cross-fertilization are best planted in a city like New Orleans or Manhattan, where people of different backgrounds live together so closely that their lives and music intertwine. A city's character evolves with each new influx of arrivals. The first wave of Cuban musicians to flee Fidel Castro and to live in New York—including singer Celia Cruz, bandleader Machito, and percussionist Chano Pozo—altered American music. After hours, Cuban musicians would improvise—a custom called *descarga*. Virtuoso bass player, composer, and bandleader, Cachao, introduced it. When Cuban musicians hit Manhattan, the affinity between Afro-Cuba's improvised *descarga* sessions and bebop's competitive jams became clear. Trumpeter Dizzy Gillespie played with Chano Pozo and Quincy Jones performed with Machito. Their synergy became known as Cu-bop. Among these significant musical encounters, a spark lit the pan-Latin flame of salsa in the 1970s. Cubans like Cruz met Puerto Rican artists like percussionist Tito Puente and Dominicans like the writer/producer Johnny Pacheco.

Decades later, Celia Cruz recorded the Cuban song "Guantanamera" on Fugees rapper Wyclef Jean's eclectic 1997 solo album *The Carnival*. "I always think of hearing "Guantanamera" when I was a little girl in the suburbs of Havana. It always made me cry,"[7] Cruz reminisced.

When Jean arrived from Haiti as a young boy, Cuban music was already integrated into the New York soundtrack. "I used to hear 'Guantanamera' where I grew up in the Marlborough Projects on Coney Island," he said nostalgically. "We'd be downstairs on the first floor, and on the second floor the Hispanics would be bumping music loud."[8]

The strains of a folk song united these very different artists across continents and generations; just as music tied together South Africa and African America.

The sophisticated jazz piano of Abdullah Ibrahim, formerly Dollar Brand, reflects how African-American culture was an inspiring emblem of freedom for South African musicians—no matter how restrictive conditions were for Harlem's jazz players. The stomp of Ibrahim's essentially South African shebeen (seedy bar) township jazz and his delicate keyboard meditations is also steeped in a lineage of American pianists. There to be heard is boogie-woogie Chicago player Pinetop Perkins, one of the first featured artists when radio was revolutionizing the blues and a member of Muddy Waters' band. Also present are jazz classic futurist Thelonious Monk and the majestic jazz sonatas and symphonies of the young Brand's mentor, Duke Ellington.

Ellington spotted Ibrahim's gift and invited him to America. Just as the young Sowetan had imagined, there were the great orchestras, musical treasure troves like Ellington's and Count Basie's featuring the urbane vocalist, Joe Williams and the trumpet of Harry 'Sweets' Edison, who graced many of Frank Sinatra's 1950s Capitol recordings. The vanguard trumpeter, Miles Davis, noted, "The way you play behind a singer is like the way Harry "Sweets" Edison did with Frank. When Frank stopped singing, Harry played. You never play over a singer."[9]

Other artists also inspired young musicians. Through four decades of different incarnations of his Jazz Messengers, drummer Art Blakey, like singer Betty Carter, mentored younger musicians. He spanned the transition from big band culture to the smaller groups of the 1960s. "I worked in all the big bands. The first thing I do, I go in and introduce myself to all the individual musicians and the soloists. And I ask them is there anything I can do to make them sound better or make them feel good."[10]

In that sense, the big bands were a model of

a functioning society, a world whose inhabitants interacted for the mutual good. For African America as a whole, the church was the central structure both spiritually and socially. In the face of degradation, the church provided a sanctuary. Initially, Christianity was foisted on Africans as a form of control, but they made it their own. Their hope and pain infused songs like the eighteenth-century English hymn "Amazing Grace." More than four hundred years later its relevance persists. The slave masters' hymn is still being sung by artists like Aretha Franklin and saxophonist David Murray and New Orleans vocalist Aaron Neville. They have all reached for glory with their interpretation of "Amazing Grace."

Enslaved African Americans reinvented the stiff Methodist and Wesleyan plaints with a feeling that in the 1970s would come to be called soul. They stretched the notes into the sort of wailing melisma later employed by Al Green and Mary J. Blige.

"If African music is the root of a tree," said Baaba Maal, "gospel and blues are two of its strongest supporting branches." The unaccompanied voices of the Vance Ensemble and the rich timbre of singer Carrie Smith perpetuate the old spirituals and the work of veterans like Mahalia Jackson. Gospel's influence spreads far beyond the church. "Vocally, I still give up the gospel feel," said rapper and producer, Missy Elliott, whose mother took her to church each Sunday. "Among entertainers I've worked with, you can tell the difference between an artist who can just sing and an artist who's come from the church; they can hear (harmonies and timing) automatically."

Gospel groups like the Staples Singers often perform as families. Though not related by blood, The Blind Boys of Alabama have been praising the Lord in various permutations since they formed at the Talladega Institute for the Deaf and Blind in Alabama in 1937. The Winans Family are a phenomenon. All their children, including Be Be, Ce Ce, Angie, Debie, Marvin, Carvin, Ronald, and Michael, are musicians and singers in different bands.

"Through the Winans, I feel the spirit, a lot," said the R&B star Monica. "They are truthfully spiritual, but they bring gospel in a form even younger people can understand. Kirk Franklin is more of a mixture."

The Family, the group of gospel's 1990s rejuvenator, Kirk Franklin, is all-inclusive. Their "Nu Nation" adopts artists who may seem dissimilar, but are nonetheless called to uplift, such as Bono of the rock band U2, and rappers Salt'n'Pepa. They all belong in the Family.

"Family is the most important thing for West Africans; we count on the people in our family for everything. Griots are travelling families," wrote Susa in *Jali Kunda*. In the blues of the Mississipi Delta, Baaba Maal recognises his role in the African diaspora. "In Mali, when they play the dousn'gouni (a hunter's guitar) they play the blues."[11]

The blues convey existential angst, tempered with survivalist humor. "The blues are a consistent part of the struggle of Black people, but they're also something personal. The essence of you, trying to sum up where you are," explained the poet and activist Jayne Cortez. Onstage with a free-flowing jazz group including her drummer son, Denardo, she chants hypnotically, "I'm the owner of the blues, from a long long time ago."

Along with a free generation eager to sample all America had to offer, blues men who grew up in the Depression left sharecropping behind to taste the bright lights and big city, among them John Lee Hooker and B.B. King. Like New Orleans before them, Memphis and Detroit became circuit boards sparking with new blues.

Although he made his name in Detroit it was to Memphis that John Lee Hooker first ran away from home and jammed with B.B. King and the elegant Bobby "Blue" Bland. They constructed the template for a second generation called electric urban blues that was edgier than the acoustic sound of the cotton fields.

Always open to experimentation, John Lee Hooker had the deepest Delta sound. His hard tapping right foot and guitar echoed the African *kora* with its shaker. So unique and in demand was Hooker's style—learned from his stepfather—that he recorded under at least ten aliases, including the apt John Lee Cooker. Briefly, Hooker employed Bobby "Blue" Bland as his valet, and indeed Bland's hairdos were always as smooth as his voice. Bland's 1950s pompadours, slick and black as a vinyl single rose to a low Afro in the 1960s. But as Jayne Cortez observed, "The hairstyle changed, but the music always stays the same." Bland's connection with the funk was embodied in his drummer, John Jabo Starks, who later joined James Brown and patented the much-sampled "funky drummer" rhythm.

The post-modern, third generation sound—a chilling minimalist telecaster axe attack sound—

Burning Spear — London 1987
Jolly Boys — Port Antonio, Jamaica 1990
Wild Magnolias — Portsmouth, England 1991
Roni Size — Bristol England 1998

**Haitian Musicians**

Port-au-Prince 1995

was delivered by Albert Collins. He was a sharecropper's son from Texas who hit it big with his first record, The Freeze. He also jammed with B.B., and the original gangster of love, Johnny "Guitar" Watson.

Collins' insouciant attitude appealed to a young guitarist named Robert Cray, who came across Collins in his parents' record collection. He had no personal experience of the rural life that shaped his inspirations. A personable young man playing the blues was a rarity, as a younger generation had turned away from this music. In his book Blues All Around Me, co-written by David Ritz, B.B. King described that

Texas guitarist Clarence "Gatemouth" Brown. Sturdily they bear radical interpretations from the "harmolodic" free jazz played by Ornette Coleman and "jazz-punk" guitarist James "Blood" Ulmer, author of the oft-quoted title, Jazz is the Teacher, Funk is the Preacher.

When people first started playing roots music, it was just music. The idea of "roots" is an urban invention, objectifying the most ancestral sources of music from a distance. In America, the "roots" concept was partly spread by the influential 1977 TV series of that name, based on the novel by Alex Haley with music by South Africans, Letta M'bulu and Caiphus Semenya. The

Jayne Cortez New York 1994
Harry "Sweets" Edison New York 19
Arrow London 1983
Courtney Pine London 1986

period: "In pushing ahead, sometimes we forget the old forms of music. They represent a time we'd rather forget . . . the blues is an expression of anger against shame or humiliation."[12] As Kirk Franklin was to do with gospel, Cray drew a new audience to blues.

"The blues is the foundation and the building block of American popular music," observed Cassandra Wilson. "Reinterpreting the blues, especially in its relation to jazz, is partly drawing upon the ancient form that still feeds us. But there's also an important process of evolution in the music, so it's a paradox. You have to return to the source to refresh yourself."

The beams and girders of the house of popular music were raised by musicians like the Chicago harmonica player Junior Wells and by the

style of roots was articulated by artists like the amiable Taj Mahal. Known as a bluesman, his empathy for African, Caribbean, and other source musics positioned him to be the first American artist to spread the "rootsical" aesthetic, initially on his influential 1977 Mo' Roots album.

With her towering headwrap, the dainty Erykah Badu brought glamour to roots. As R&B players with gospel roots talk about taking it to church, Badu makes the stage a shrine. "I use incense and candles on stage to build a bridge to understanding." Almond-shaped eyes gleaming, Badu answered journalists' questions in Jamaica at the 1997 Montego Bay Jazz and Blues Festival, "The headwrap has been a symbol of African beauty for me since high school. Though I don't claim any religion, I guess I am a witch of

Art Blakey New York 1985

Abdullah Ibrahim (Dollar Brand) Bracknell, England 1982

London 1981

# Fats

# Domino

35

sorts—in a positive way."

A look can send a message. Assured in her queenly African headwraps, Aretha Franklin recorded "Amazing Grace" in her father's church in the Civil Rights era. The headwrap's flattering dignity was revived again a decade later by the high stepping I-Three's, Bob Marley's back-up trio. Leading Jamaican singers Rita Marley, Judy Mowatt, and Marcia Griffith gladly merged their skills to sing with "Jah B," and Mowatt made the evergreen female Jamaican message record, *Black Woman*.

Like enslaved Africans in America, the people in Jamaica during slavery were poorly fed

It intertwines African heritage with European dances like the quadrille, Irish jigs and reels, and with the austere structure of Wesleyan hymns that in America were informing gospel and blues.

The enslaved Africans who arrived in Jamaica came from West Africa's Fon, Yoruba, Coromantees, and Manding groups, whose traditions molded African music stars like Salif Keita and Youssou N'Dour some five hundred years later. They brought with them the animism that translated into obeah and the funde, repeater, and kete drums whose insistent patterns still echo electronically in the digital dancehall music of reggae's Rhythm Twins, Sly and Robbie.

Carrie Smith New York 1998

Vance Ensemble New York 1998

and severely whipped. Ultimately, the island that suffered and struggled so hard became the main global transmitter of the ideas of rebel music—notably, socially conscious reggae music popularized by Bob Marley and Burning Spear in the 1970s and Luciano and Anthony B in the 1990s.

The folk music that predated independence, *mento*, held echoes of Jamaica's first Spanish conquerors. The Jolly Boys bamboo saxophone recalls the bamboo fiddles the Tainos or Arawak Indians used to play. This ethnic group was entirely eliminated by Spanish colonizers less than two hundred years after Christopher Columbus' 1494 arrival.

The Jamaican motto is "Out of many, one people," and that principle applies to their music.

The African drums were kept alive by the Kumina and Pocomania religions and in the all-night grounation *nyabinghi* drumming sessions of the Rastafarian encampments in the Wareika Hills. Groups like the late Count Ossie and the Mystic Revelation of Rastafari and Ras Michael and the Sons of Negus invoke the downfall of the oppressors.

The intriguing Rastafarian idea of a Black god, Ethiopia's Emperor Haile Selassie, swept through the rough Kingston squatter settlements in the 1930s. Asked why he was a Rasta, Bob Marley flashed a look of exasperation. "You want me to worship a white god?"[13] he asked incredulously.

African rhythms long guarded by the Maroons began to be heard in the shantytowns and tenement yards. Folklore experts recorded the drumming and chanting and passed it on.

The American bebop and New Orleans R&B barrelhouse boogie-woogie they were picking up from short wave radios excited Jamaican musicians. Although the sound was often distorted by static, they began to synthesize the sounds and made a music named—after its choppy guitar downbeat—ska. "I used to travel to New Orleans to look for records," recalled Coxsone Dodd in his studio at Maxfield Avenue, where Bob Marley used to sleep when times were rough. Other artists who recorded at Studio One are a roll call of reggae greatness, including the Heptones, Freddie McGregor, Dennis Brown, singer-songwriter Bob Andy, and Burning Spear.

"It was a college. All the people who went through Clement Dodd's (Coxsone's) school did well after a while,"[14] recalled Burning Spear. "Me and Bob (Marley) used to have some nice reasoning in the hills—we both come from St. Anns, y'know."

Bob Marley, Peter Tosh, and Bunny Wailer were the original Wailers. Known as the "rude boys," their group briefly included a woman named Beverley Kelso. They met up living in the "government yards" (subsidized housing developments) down by the sea in Kingston's Trenchtown ghetto. Their songs glorified underdogs, rebels, street fighting, and teenage jailbirds which is illustrated in the lyrics of Tosh's "I'm the Toughest" and "Rudy Get Bail," among other songs.

As the group evolved, so did Jamaican pop: from kitschy cover songs like "What's New Pussycat" (the 1960s comedy film theme tune originally sung by Tom Jones) to *nyabinghi* drum chants; ska; psychedelia; the slower, more sensuous rock steady; and prototypical, spaced-out dub—in their work with the visionary producer Lee Perry. Their maturation became a yardstick of Jamaica's independent identity and growth.

Eventually, Peter Tosh struck out alone and Bunny Wailers retreated to his farm in Bull Bay, releasing albums irregularly. It was left to the roots-rock reggae of Bob Marley to steer reggae to global awareness.

**The Winans** London 1986

**Blind Boys of Alabama** New York 1998

The Wailers became the most internationally prominent example of one of Jamaican music's greatest treasures, its harmony trio tradition. Performed in unison or African call and response style, voices blend and weave, demonstrating the highest level of human exchange.

Contemporaries of the young Wailers, Toots and the Maytals made sanctified roots. Toots', "The Ska Father," grainy voice embraced gospel and the old obeah rituals that are conducted alongside Christianity.

Harmony meant a mysterious glide through half-tones and minor plaints for the Abyssinians. Their haunting tune, "Satta Massagana," beseeches, "Get up and fight for your rights, my brother, my sister." They used the Ethiopian Amharic language to evoke pre-slavery days, yearning for a lost homeland, and implying ultimate endurance.

Patti LaBelle

London 1986

**Kirk Franklin**
New York 1998

Originally part of a trio, Burning Spear took his name from that of Kenyan rebel leader, Jomo Kenyatta. On tracks like "Door Peep (shall not enter)" and "Rocking Time," his dry sound suggested Africa's red deserts.

Spear's theme song became "Marcus Garvey." In identifying himself so intimately with the philosopher and visionary activist Marcus Garvey, Spear was promoting another St. Ann's Bay man. Garvey preached a gospel of pride and self-reliance, developing his philosophy of repatriation that would encourage descendants of enslaved Africans back to Africa. Holding fast to his beliefs, Garvey died in poverty in London, but his ideas became ever more influential.

In communicating history so directly, Spear extended a tradition not only of the African griots but of the medieval jongleurs and troubadours who roamed Europe spreading news. They were the CNN of their day, to paraphrase hip hoppers Public Enemy's self-description.

Nowhere in the Caribbean was the griot's lineage more pronouced than in Trinidad. Though its music is flavored by the tassa drums of its Indian population and their brand of "chutney" pop, the island is most famous for its steel pan and calypso. Satirizing everything, particularly the government, calypso artists like Gypsy, Superblue, and Machel Montano rival each other with anthems for every carnival. Appreciation of their humor and insight is island-wide and their songs are dissected by the public as eagerly as sport fans analyzing teams.

The supremacy of calypso pioneers such as Lord Kitchener, the eleven-time carnival march winner, and the Mighty Sparrow, was challenged in the 1980s by a politically conscious Rastafarian named Black Stalin.

But few artists have enjoyed the longevity of the dapper Roaring Lion, known for sporting a sharp suit and cane. The gravel voice of the "Papa Chunks Man" has spanned the birth of the industry. In 1934, he cut his first calypso recording in Manhattan with his partner, Attila the Hun. Papa experienced a revival of his career at seventy, backed by hardcore Trinidadian players, like the laid-back veteran bandleader and saxophonist Roy Cape.

The producer who steered the Roaring Lion's unique comeback with his tumbling "ring-bang" rhythm was Guyanan-born, England-raised Eddy Grant. As a teenager sporting a trademark blond Afro with his group the Equals, Grant became the first Black British pop star with the funky bubblegum of "Baby Come Back." He went on to score solo with hits like "Walking On Sunshine" and "Electric Avenue." Success enabled him to pursue his calypso obsession and revive the career of Roaring Lion, Black Stalin, and Calypso Rose, "The Mother of Calypso," with his label, Ice Records.

Among the synthesized drums in Grant's "ring-bang" rhythm was an old Manding beat that also became popular in 1990s Jamaican dancehall, a sexy two-drop called "boom-boom." In reggae, the top session drummer king, Sly Dunbar, of the Sly and Robbie Rhythm Killers duo, started experimenting with synthesized drums as soon as they became available. Electronic drum beats soon became a staple of reggae as they were of all the new forms of dance music like Chicago house and Detroit techno.

In a faceless DJ genre like techno, the melodic sense of Bristol's Roni Size made him an original. He remembers the birth of the "junglist" scene, "A combination of Black music and celebrations like the carnivals in London's Notting Hill and Bristol's St. Paul's. In the rave scene, it was about partying in the field;

**Cassandra Wilson**

New York 1999

whether you were Black or White didn't matter, it was a bit of both.

"But the two turntables and a mixer, setting up a sound system in a field, is a Black idea."

The multicultural junglists raving at dawn in a green West Country meadow may seem removed from Africa, but as they say in Jamaica, the fruit never falls far from the tree. "The speed of jungle reminds me of our ceremonies where the speed builds up and gets very hot towards the end, and the women dancing start to freestyle."

British drum'n'bass renegade Goldie was formed by many influences, including a hip-hop period spent as a graffiti artist following Afrika Bambaata's Zulu Nation in the Bronx.

"I've zoomed in on the drums, making African drum loops, right against the cutting edge of technology," he reported. "I'm lucky. I have five generations of music that I can draw from and zoom in on by using a sample. For me, it's blues, Detroit techno, reggae, New York b-boy music and drum'n'bass.

"Everything comes from the black chord—the Beatles, rock'n'roll. It's been held through time, but it was really captured with recordable audio, when people began to loop it, and take things from it. That's when music of Black origin becomes the black chord."

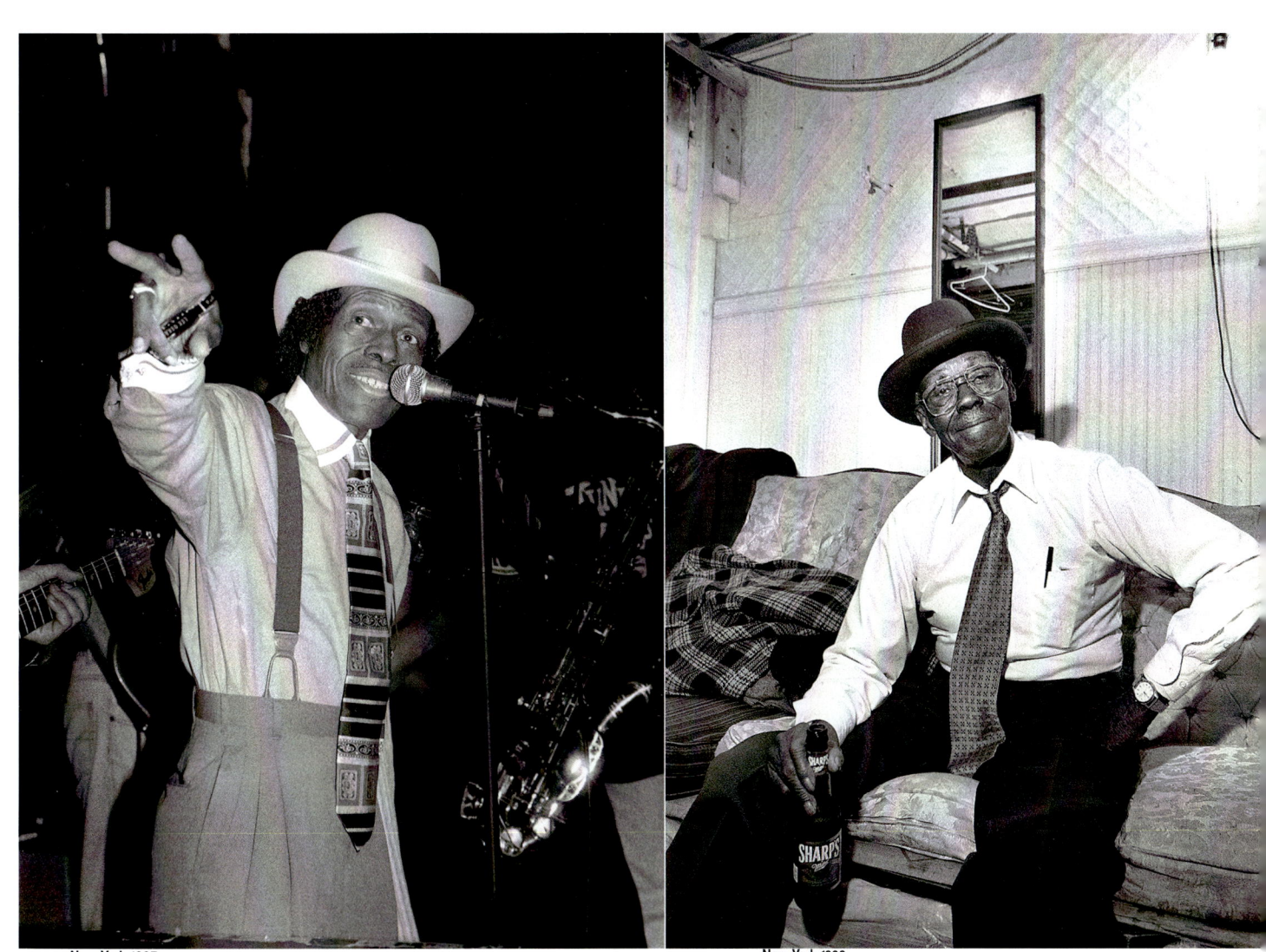

Jr. Wells **New York 1997**

Pinetop Perkins **New York 1998**

John Lee Hooker

London 1982

Albert Collins London 1979

James "Blood" Ulmer London 1981

Taj Mahal London 1987

Eddie Grant London 1980

London 1982

# B.B. King

44

Wynton Marsalis

New York 1999

45

Following page: Robert Cray London 1985

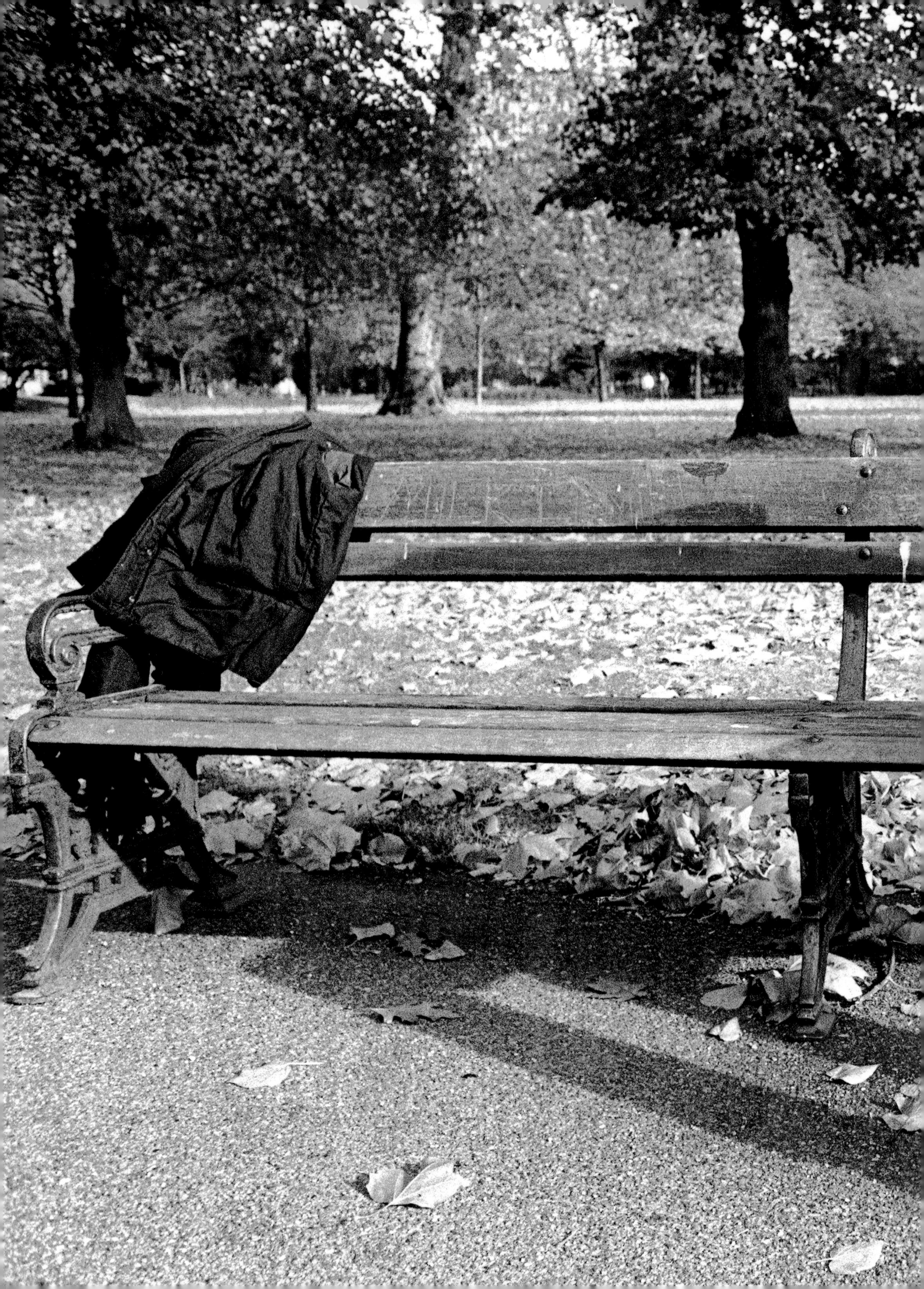

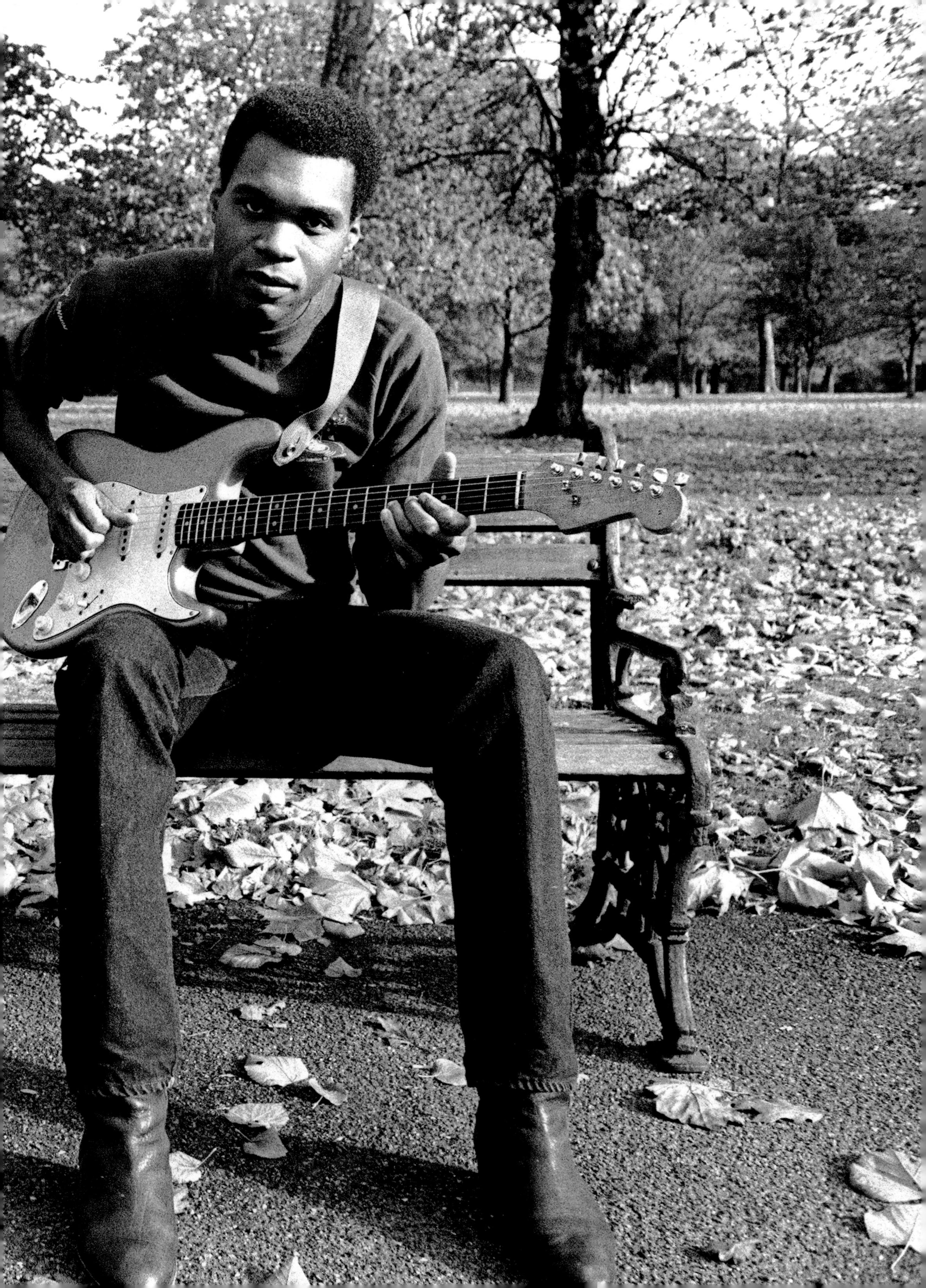

This page clockwise from top: Marcia Griffiths, London 1990; Judy Mowatt, London 1987; Rita Marley, New York 1993 Opposite page: Erykah Badu (top), New York 1997; Abyssinians, London

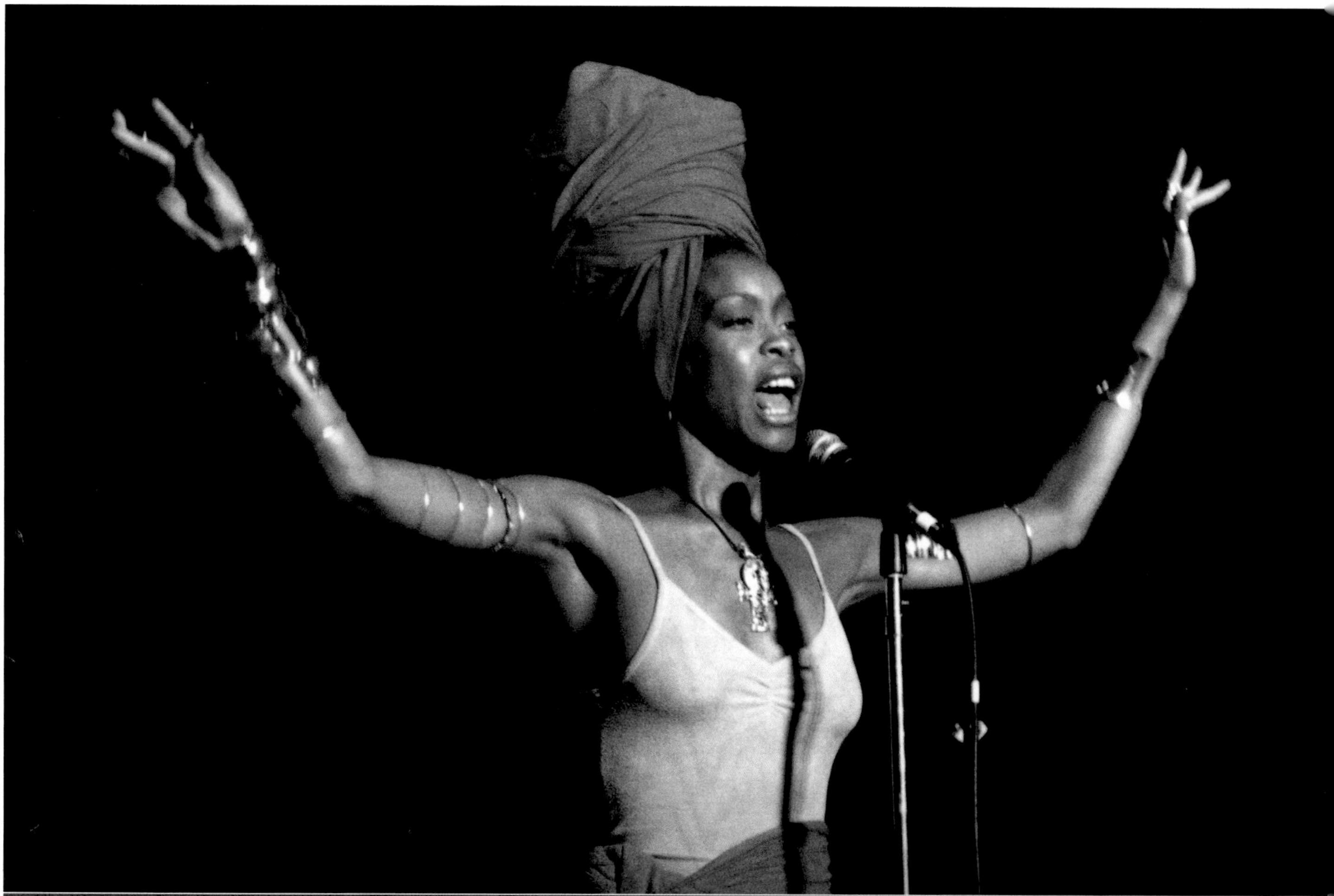
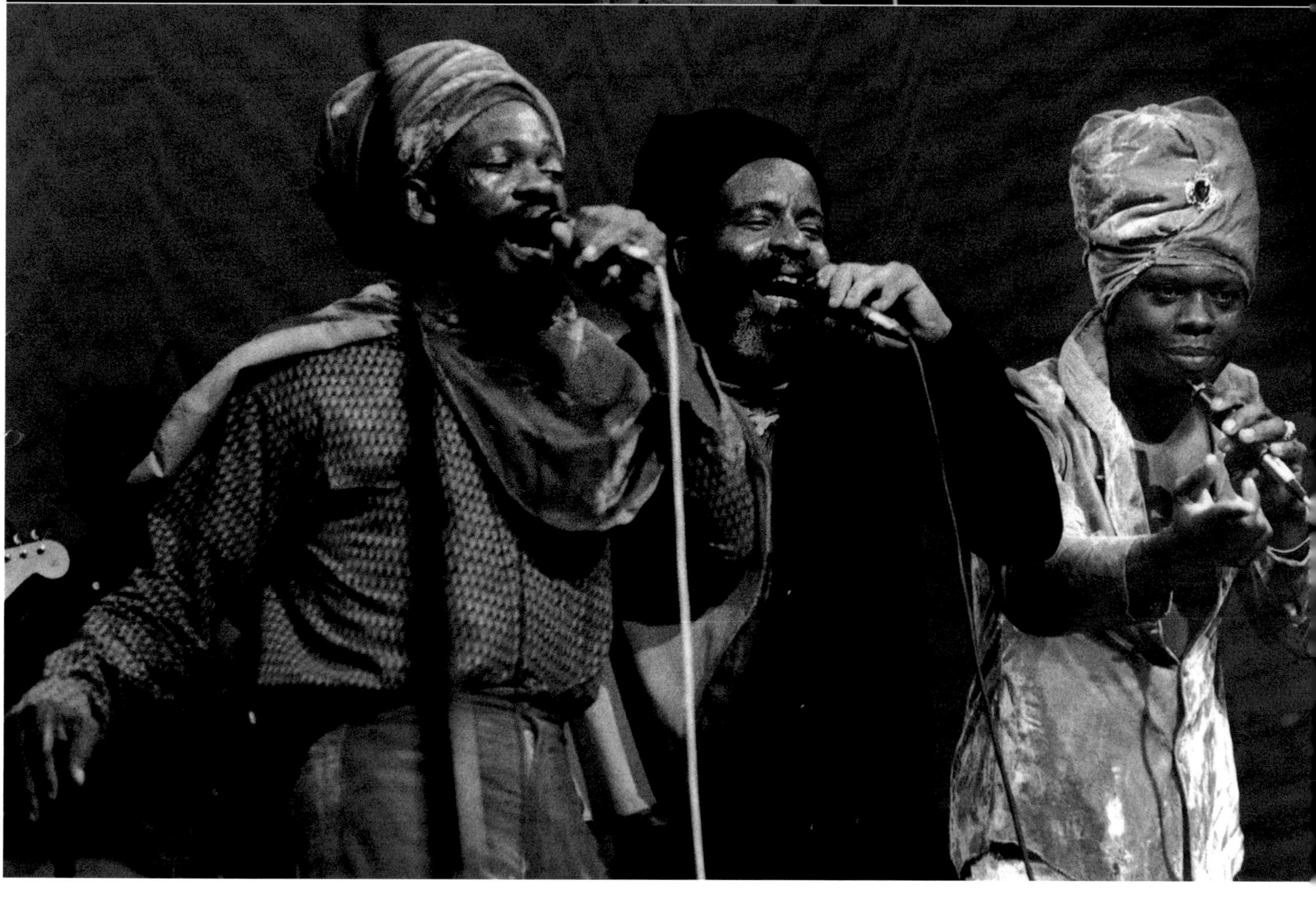

**Roaring Lion** Port of Spain, Trinidad 1990

**Roy Cape** Port of Spain, Trinidad 1990

**Bunny Wailer** London 1988

**Black Stalin** Port of Spain, Trinidad 1990

Goldie
London 1998

heat

London 1984 — Al Green

# HEART & SOUL

# soul

Popular music has always been in love with love. In the early days of recording, love songs turned people on with erotic euphemisms. Blues Empress Bessie Smith needed a little sugar in her bowl, and Robert Johnson wanted his lemon squeezed 'til the juice ran down his leg. When Jamaican songs of the 1960s talked about the big bamboo and the banana, they weren't referring to farming.

But over the years, social and sexual conditions have shifted radically, and with them, the way music talks about love. "You used to make songs where things were implied or assumed. Now you have to be blatantly honest, because people switch songs to their own meaning," said R&B singer Monica.

When a boyfriend got another woman pregnant, Monica and producer Dallas Austin turned the trauma into a song. "I had to be at peace with myself before I could even sing about it. Once I was at peace, I wanted every other woman in the same situation to know it's not their fault." The directness of her lyrics alarmed her record label, but aware of the heavy sexual pressure on young girls, Monica insisted on singing it how she sees it. "You can't twist that!" she laughed with satisfaction of upfront cautionary lines like "Boy, you didn't use protection."

The black chord binds all kinds of love, depicting and provoking extremes of pleasure and pain. Its love songs explain our feelings to others and ourselves when our own words let us down. As wildman Parliament Funkadelic bassist Bootsy Collins observed of his languorous track "I Got The Munchies For Your Love," "It's probably made a lot of new babies."[15]

Romantic love is not the only kind of love Black musicians expressed in song. Since the first African griot ardently chanted the praises of his local monarch, all the variations of love humans can feel have been articulated in music: love of community and country, love of family, adoration of material things, and a yearning for a supreme being.

In the African praise song tradition, it is not the singer's place to criticize or pass moral judgement. The sacred, traditional function is to flatter, to "big up."

Rooted in the praise song tradition, Nigeria's many musical rhythms like fuju and juju energize with hypnotic ranks of massed percussion, the eloquent gulp of the Yoruba talking drum, and, in the case of King Sunny Ade, the Hawaiian steel guitar.

In the 1980s, the early days of the world music genre, Ade's experiments with electric juju—like the track "Ja Funmi," along with other crossover hits by Mory Kante and Manu Dibango—made African music accessible to international club kids. Generally associated with the wealthy and the ruling class, the genial King Sunny's earlier local 1970s hits include a tribute to the late General Murtala Muhammed, the Nigerian dictator.

Since he fronted the Rail Band of Bamako in the 1960s, one of the most enduring songs in Malian Salif Keita's repertoire has remained "Mandjou," a tribute epic dedicated to Sekou Touré, the man who steered Guinea from colonialism to independence. As the only new African leader to refuse dependency on France, their former colonizer, Touré was lauded by all revolutionaries. Unfortunately, his separatism hardened into autocracy, and his tyrannical regime forced a generation into exile. Nonetheless, Touré set up significant music and dance programs as Mobutu did in Zaire. He offered a home to dispossessed artists and revolutionaries like

Kwame Toure, formerly Stokeley Carmichael—the Black Panther who coined the cry "Black Power"—and his South African wife, singer Miriam Makeba.

Keita was among those who were always welcome in the Palais de la Révolution in Conakry. Asked why he sang in praise of a tyrant, Keita answered wryly, "Sure, Sekou Touré was a dictator, but he was still a nice guy."

Loyalty to a neighborhood has spilled blood, but it has also stirred paeans to community unity. When Toots and the Maytals recorded "Funky Kingston" in 1973, they were announcing that the Jamaican capital was not a backward, bush place, but rather a groovy metropolis with vibes to rival Harlem's. While ethnic warfare ripped apart Kingston's shanty towns in 1976, Bob Marley wrote "Smile Jamaica," a song as chirpy as a tourist-board advertisement and much different than the Rasta revolutionary's usual militant style. Why? Swigging a roots drink in his own Tuff Gong recording studio in Kingston, Marley tossed back his locks and growled, "De people in Jamaica too vex, mon."

Days later, before the song had a chance to soothe the people, Marley was shot by downtown dons, then went into exile after playing a Peace Concert.

Whether it's a political, public, private, or family affair, the same types of love engage people everywhere, though with some significant regional variations.

Tribute songs to mother and familial love are a perennial favorite and are as different from one another as families. Natalie Cole reunited digitally with her late father, Nat King Cole, for a duet on his song "Unforgettable." A tender love song to her then unborn child, "Zion" was Lauryn Hill's prenatal gift on her album, *The Miseducation of Lauryn Hill*. The Intruders suggest a happy home as they affirm, "I'll Always Love My Mama" and Goldie's cut "Mother" is a CD-long primal scream.

A generation of rebel female singers and griots have co-opted the traditional *wassoullou* vocal sound from Mali and Senegal to make controversial commentary on love and marriage. Though polygamy is common in Mali, as in other Muslim countries, it is a tradition criticized by artists such as the dynamic Oumou Sangare. Her bright, keening wail, on her album *Ko Sira*, draws attention to the pain she experienced in a polygamous family.

Known as "Madame Chic-Choc" (Mrs. Chic and Shocking) for her combination of glamour and shock value, Guinean singer Oumou Dioubate scandalized the country with her song "Lancey" produced by Ibrahim Sylla. In it Dioubate reveals the secret, ritual fertility dance that childless women perform called *Moribadjassa*. Dioubate's courage and candor alienated her from society and from her husband, who eventually left her.

Another grim prognosis of romantic relationships was sung by Malian Bi Funi in her

Weathergirls  New York 1985

Four Tops  London 1985

# Youssou N'Dour

London 1988

Barry White  London 1988

59

track "Sigi Kurun" (Modern Marriage): "You, the woman I am talking to, when your husband's brother beats you, do not attach any importance to it, and especially do not answer back. To each our destiny." Rapper RZA of the Wu Tang Clan echoes this brutal analysis of relationships on his track "Domestic Violence." The song features a violently realistic shouting match between a couple.

The theme of brutal love is nothing new. In "Yes Indeed He Do," blues woman Bessie Smith faithfully chronicles both the fear and the ugly erotic bond in abusive relationships: "I said for fun I don't want you no more. And when I said that I made sweet papa sore. He blacked my eye, I couldn't see. Then he pawned the things he gave to me. But outside of that, he's alright with me."

The blues, the first music of free African Americans, was juicy. Blues marked the end of slavery, during which men and women's sexuality was not their own. Both sexes were used for breeding at plantation owners' commands. From this grimly unromantic heritage, Black Americans created a canon of love songs that's been adopted over the world.

Smokey Robinson, the original leader of the Miracles and Motown's love bard, launched a sensuous musical genre with his delicate poetry titled, *A Quiet Storm* after his first solo record.

In his autobiography, *Inside My Life*, co-authored by David Ritz, Smokey recalled his father sharing their family history while they were on a fishing trip. "Owners turned [your grandfather] into a stud. Many a time they'd order him to mate with their prettiest lady slaves. Wanted 'em to turn out perfect kids to sell for big money."[16]

Emancipation meant that Smokey's grandfather was able to marry the woman he loved and bear twelve free children, including Smokey's father.

For artists, understanding the chemistry of love is important, especially to singer Barry White. White uses his low-down growl as an oratorical hot-oil massage. From an adolescent gangbanger, White matured into a musical orchestrator of his audience's fantasies. Putting on a Barry White track meant "putting out," an invitation to a horizontal conversation. "The lyrics, the melodies, the music. You know, when people are slow dancing, they hear everything. When they're by themselves with the person that they want to be with, there are certain songs that fit those occasions. I always wanted to have one of those songs that fits any occasion," said White.

That ability to adapt is essential for artists whose work straddles the spiritual and the secular—or the sexual. An image of the solid family man, aching to work things out with his soul mate, is evident in Levi Stubbs and the Four Tops' 1960s soul; Ben E. King's singing "Stand By Me" in 1961; and Will Downing's croon in the 1990s. Others are torn by the tension between body and soul.

In the work of artists like Al Green and R. Kelly, that duality merges. At the music's height, as when Al Green's ethereal vibrato stretches the vamp of "Let's Get Married," it sounds like heaven. Erotic and spiritual love fuse into one conflicted notion: "It's you I want but Him that I need."

The Reverend Al Green preaches in Memphis, continuing a life's work first began at eight years old in church with his three brothers William, Walter, and Robert. In many church circles, anything other than gospel was known as "the devil's music," and Al was much criticized when in 1964 he formed a pop group, the Creations. Green found his sound when record producer Willie Mitchell generated a series of memorable 1970s albums teaming Al's eloquent voice with sparse, steamy arrangements laced with horns.

"'Bout five o'clock one Friday morning, I was sittin' up on the side of my bed, 'cause I'm a bachelor, you see," Green told *Black Music* magazine in the 1970s, "and I said to myself, 'I'm so tired of being alone.'"[17] He transformed his early morning blues into a song that epitomizes yearning. However, after a woman scalded him with a pan of grits, Al Green rededicated himself to the church for many years.

In 1980, wearing a flasher's raincoat, Prince came on the music scene like a comet with "Dirty Mind." The glimpse of his lean body beneath his costume was suggestive, and his lyrics were specific. His music was all designed to please the crowd and simulated masturbation, oral sex, and more. He pushed the envelope. Onstage Prince stripped and teased. Separated from his family, he reinvented himself, from pouting stud to master of his destiny, by building a recording studio in his hometown of Minneapolis and churning out hit bands and albums. In his struggle for liberation, he marked the word "slave" on his forehead in 1993 to describe his relationship with his record company, Warner

# Will Downing

New York 1993

Brothers. Once free, he was reborn as the Artist, marketed his music on the Internet, and surrounded himself with artists he had long admired, such as Mavis Staples, Larry Graham, George Clinton, and Maurice White. Like Michael Jackson, the Artist completed his transformation by getting married and becoming a Jehovah's Witness.

The voice of the prolific producer and songwriter R. Kelly throbs. The Chicago-born overachiever, who grew up in public housing, tussled with similar temptations as Green and the Artist Formerly Known as Prince. Not content with traditional erotic foreplay, on his first album R. Kelly came up with "Twelveplay," a map to working your female partner's erogenous zones. Author of "Bump 'N' Grind" and "Sex Me," Kelly's risque image was enhanced by a single he produced that was tantalizingly entitled "Age Ain't Nothing But A Number." The song was understood by some as a reference to the rumored love affair between Kelly and his gifted teenage protégé, Aaliyah, who duly became his wife, until her father broke it up.

Kelly learned to ride the big bang of raunch and religion. Born again as a Christian, he recorded the uplifting anthem "I Believe I Can Fly," and prayed in song with gospel artist Kirk Franklin.

The content of their music doesn't necessarily reflect godly preoccupations, but sometimes a sense of purpose is apparent in the disparate sounds of such preachers' children as Aretha Franklin, Marvin Gaye, experimental soul singer Terence Trent D'Arby, neo-soul man D'Angelo, and the Fugees' Wyclef.

The clichéd connotations of being a preacher's son can sometimes prove to be just a con. Trying to keep him straight, Wyclef's preacher father would beat him for staying out late to make music. Marvin Gaye's preacher father gave him life, then—because he disapproved of Marvin's crossdressing—took it away with a gun the day before Marvin was scheduled to begin work on a new album with Barry White.

A sensitive sensualist, Gaye always asked the philosophical questions in his music that tormented him in life. He confronted hardcore sexual reality with orgasmic songs like "I Want You," and "Sexual Healing" (co-written with David Ritz). When his singing partner, Tammi Terrell, collapsed in his arms onstage and later died, he withdrew from recording. He eventually returned with the revolutionary consciousness of the groundbreaking soul protest album *What's Going On*. Forced to make a record to pay alimony to his ex-wife Anna—the sister of Motown label chief, Berry Gordy—Gaye responded with a directness even she had to feel: "When did I stop loving you, when did you stop loving me?" on his song titled, "Here My Dear."

"If you're gonna make love and do these things that in some societies are considered deviant, then let's make it an honest situation,"[18] Gaye explained earnestly.

There have been many great love singers, each with their own style of romancing. None seem as driven as Gaye. The mellow sound of Gaye's own protégé Frankie Beverly, from the band Maze, projected a balanced, optimistic lover. Beverly seems well-adjusted, like he always gets the girl, it's just a question of when. Gaye was still wracked with anxiety even after he got her.

Love can be transformative. Aaron Neville looks tough, but his tender falsetto and melting eyes have made him a romantic lead ever since he sang "Tell It Like It Is," in 1966. Lionel Ritchie is another romantic singer. Ritchie sang hard-driving funk with the Commodores in the 1970s, but his melodic songs became so popular that the group instead became known for sentimental ballads like "Three Times a Lady." Solo, Ritchie went on to record soft-funk narratives like "Running With The Night" and "All Night Long" that invested romance with drama.

Voices once dedicated to gospel's divine passion have stirred earthly urges ever since Sam Cooke left his gospel group the Soul Stirrers and "crossed over" to R&B. Cooke's butterfly-kiss voice didn't just sing "You Send Me," it seduced. Cooke became the first crossover African-American pop star, dubbed the "Sepia Sinatra." Boldly setting up his own independent label, Sar Records, he discovered a talented band called the Valentinos. The group featured Bobby Womack, who also doubled as guitarist in Sam's band, as he would later do with Aretha Franklin and Ray Charles.

Womack's music projects the robust, virile

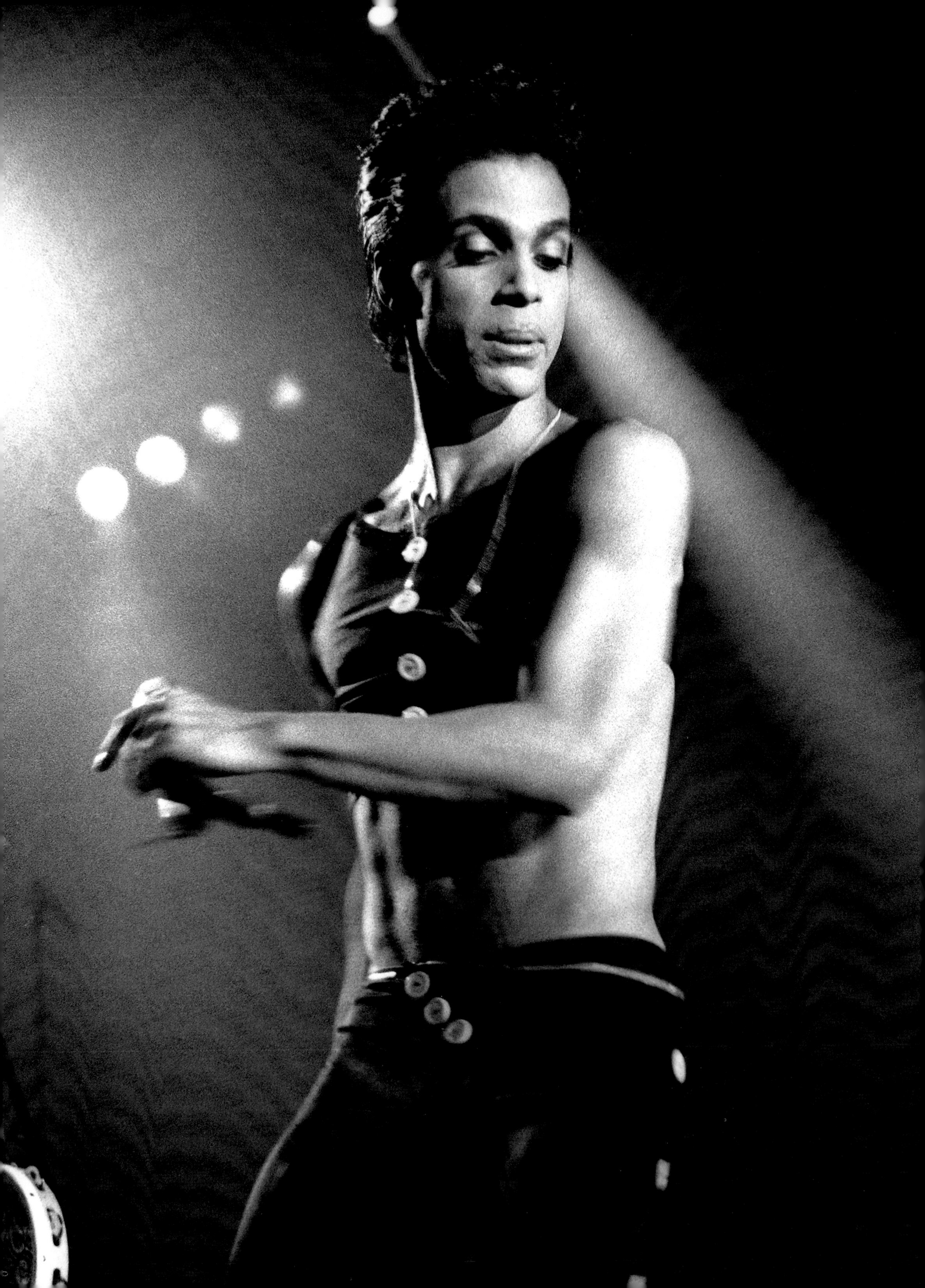

Terence Trent D'arby London 1987

presence of a party animal on tracks like "Daylight," with its amused admission, "Most people are getting up when I'm just getting in." Known first as the Preacher, then the Poet, Womack's earthy voice ministers to all his listeners' needs, healing and releasing angelic and carnal desires. Bobby Womack sounds unshockable, like he's seen and done it all. Knowingly, he sings, "If you think you're lonely now, wait until tonight, girl."

Sitting in a hotel suite in 1976, Womack reminisced, "I used to tell him [Sam Cooke], 'Hey man, you can't go down and mingle with the people. Man, you ain't part of them any more.' And he'd say, 'No, I am a part of them, they'd never hurt me.' And he'd get out of his car and stand on a corner. I'd say, 'Man, I'm surprised you walked that corner.' Normally them thugs would've whipped him. He just had a lot of nerve."[19]

Touched by the Civil Rights Movement, Cooke made his most socially aware recording, "A Change Is Gonna Come." It proved to be his last. He was shot by Bertha Franklin, the owner of the Hacienda Motel in Los Angeles, who alleged he'd attacked her. Three weeks after his death, Womack married Cooke's widow, Barbara, further tangling a family tree that includes the soul group Womack and Womack—the husband and wife duo of Sam Cooke's daughter Linda and Bobby's brother Cecil.

In his gospel years, Cooke, was influenced by Detroit's flamboyant, charismatic preacher, the Rev. C. L. Franklin, who spread the message on both a weekly radio show and to packed church services. The elegant young Cooke gave piano lessons to the Reverend's daughter, Aretha. She adored him. "He wore me down. Oooh, I just loved him. That man could mess up a whole room full of women,"[20] she said.

In advancing the blend of gospel and R&B that birthed soul music, Cooke's example encouraged Franklin to cross over from gospel.

Although her mother left when Aretha was a little girl, the large Franklin home was always full of people. It served as a salon, where she could absorb the aura of frequent guests such as gospel great Clara Ward, who would share insights with Aretha while cooking greens in the kitchen. Her influence worked. The term "diva," first taken from Italian opera, grew to be a tag for formidable female vocalists, but it was Aretha, with her appropriately tempestuous temperament and talent, who first earned that accolade.

Even more remarkable than Franklin's four-octave range, is her ability to reinvent herself as an emblem for every era. Franklin's first experiments outside gospel were varied, as producers tried to channel the elemental force of her voice into jazz standards and show tunes. When producer Jerry Wexler put her together with the Muscle Shoals, session musicians in Alabama, Franklin finally found her true context. It was the first of many settings in which her jewel of a voice would shine.

Together, they cut landmark songs that signalled a modern woman's desires. Black Power was on the rise alongside the stirrings of the Women's Movement, and Franklin called for love with equality in her songs, "You Make Me Feel Like (A Natural Woman)," "Do Right Man," and above all, "R.E.S.P.E.C.T." "That girl stole my

# Prince Charles

London 1981

London 1980 **Marvin Gaye**

song," its writer and original singer, Otis Redding, was known to groan, albeit with pride.

Throughout her career, Franklin has worked closely with a golden female circle, starting with her songwriter sister Carolyn, and forging forward three decades to the late '90s with the Fugees' Lauryn Hill. Catchy yet profound, their 1998 collaboration on "A Rose Is Still a Rose" upped the ante from the initial demand for respect. The lyrics stated, "Baby girl, you've got the power"—whether or not the guy's up to the job of sticking around.

Inspired by the great blues and gospel singers, Franklin's female circle continued the dynasty. Her beloved backup singer, gospel woman Cissy Houston—Dionne Warwick's cousin and leader of the Sweet Inspirations quartet—often brought her daughter Whitney to work. Being mentored by these great mothers of music was effective.

Enormously gifted, by her late teens the industry was ready to market Whitney in a way it never did for either her mother or Franklin. "Whitney was the young Black American hero for a lot of years," says Monica. "There's so many of us now—Aaliyah, Brandy, Lauryn—but in 1980, there was no one but Whitney who could sell ten or fifteen million records and be so successful. And still, you could look at the color of her skin and the smile on her face and know she was a young Black woman that had experienced the things I had."[21]

If Franklin's women were vibrant with hard-won self-assurance, Curtis Mayfield's guys were suitably evolved partners. One of Franklin's special associates, Mayfield produced her album *Sparkle*. It's hit, "Giving Him Something He Can Feel," suggests the sensuality of sexual gratification. On Mayfield's *New World Order* CD,

Whitney Houston London 1988

Bobby Womack London 1984

68

Lionel Ritchie — Birmingham, England 1987

Kingston, Jamaica 1993

Lady Saw

69

Brandy **New Jersey 1995**

R. Kelly  New York 1994

Curtis Mayfield

London 1983

Frankie Beverley London 1985

Bill Withers Los Angeles 1985

Luther Vandross London 1987

Rick James Los Angeles 1985

Teddy Riley of Blackstreet New Jersey 1996

Kenneth "Babyface" Edmonds New York 1998

recorded in 1996, some years after the singer was paralyzed in an onstage accident, Franklin sings a bravura back-up and triumphantly declares, "Go 'head Mayfield!"

Mayfield and the Impressions came of age in the 1950s doo-wop days, when street-corner harmonies soared on demurely ambiguous, virginal songs like the Penguins' 1954 hit "Earth Angel." But Mayfield's music was evolved in its emotional truth. His persona shone with the progressive chivalry of a Black man whose identity had blossomed in the Civil Rights Era.

Raised in Chicago's notorious Cabrini Green public housing facilities, Mayfield says, "My achievements have really been the success of my mother's dream. She was the artist. But my father left when she was a woman with young children and the time was not right for her. It wasn't easy, but she showed me my first little song on the piano, 'Clair de Lune.'"

Powered by a dynamic female lineage—his grandmother was a preacher and spiritual healer—Mayfield was moved to write conscientious love songs, like "Woman's Got Soul" and "I'm So Proud (to be loved by you)," that put women on a different kind of pedestal than those of doo-wop days. His women were not untouchable ideals but inspiring partners.

For Luther Vandross, "It was always the female singers who lit my fire: Aretha Franklin, Diana Ross, and Dionne Warwick were my three big idols as I was growing up,"[22] he reminisced. Vandross grew to work with all his ideal divas and collaborated with Warwick, previously known for her elegant interpretations of classy tracks such as "Do You Know the Way to San José."

First heard professionally on top-dollar radio jingles, Vandross was soon singing and writing for artists like David Bowie on his song "Young Americans." Vandross was clearly too hot not to go solo. Though a self-described "melancholic personality," so smooth is Vandross' voice that even when he beseeches and bares his anguished soul, he never loses his cool.

In contrast, manly vulnerability quivers in every note sung by Bill Withers. Unpretentious album titles like *Still Bill* and *Just As I Am* evidence Withers' pride in being a regular guy. Withers knows about work. His grandfather was a slave, his father a Virginia coal miner, and Withers himself started out in the United States Navy.

Everyday, universal longings emerge in his deceptively simple love songs. Tender empathy makes him seem like a friend and brother as well as a lover, whether encouraging, "Lean on me, when you're not strong"; appreciating the careworn contours of "Grandma's Hands": or pumping urgent lust into the refrain "Use me—until you've used me up."

The wilder extremes of love are advertised by artists like 1980s funky flute-player Prince Charles, who flashed leather fetish gear onstage. And as a self-proclaimed Super Freak, Rick James made no secret of his unusual sexual tastes. His "Fire And Desire" duet with Teena Marie suggests flashes of pleasure and pain. James' eventual jail term was the result of drugs and sex games pushed too far.

There is a constant need for romantic music, for ballads sung by an attractive voice. But both public taste and record company marketing budgets are volatile. Hip-hop began its commercial ascent, and eventually overtook rock-'n'roll in 1998. Its street-tough attitude made the elegantly dressed, conventional soul balladeers seem irrelevant to hardcore rap fans. The void was filled by the creator of New Jack Swing, Teddy Riley, who welded the hard-edged energy of hip hop to the expansive texture of gospel voices. First with his group, Guy, then with Blackstreet and as producer of many other artists, Riley linked cultures and generations.

Other producers soon crossed the bridge that Riley built, such as Sean "Puffy" Combs in the 1990s; Jimmy Jam and Terry Lewis—the former Prince sidemen whose Minneapolis studio became a conveyor belt for hits from Janet Jackson; and another producer duo, L. A. Reid and Kenneth "Babyface" Edmonds. Reid and Edmonds' teamwork framed the rich gospel feel of artists, like Boyz II Men, Whitney Houston, and her husband, Bobby Brown, in a sleek pop-edged sound. Their independent move to set up a label, LaFace, in Atlanta, helped the city become the R&B center of America with bands like the female harmony group, TLC. After their partnership ended, Babyface spread his rosy perception of love across popular culture in soundtracks—the best-selling *The Bodyguard* with Whitney Houston, *Waiting To Exhale*, and wholesome movies, like *Soul Food*.

The rap milieu is generally not conducive to the romance of Babyface. The Wu Tang Clan's rapping gang of "monks" do not project tenderness in their armory of skills, but one Clan member was not too shy to show a little love. Method Man, who became famous as a family man with "All I Need," a 1995 track remixed by Sean "Puffy" Combs, that celebrates his love for his girlfriend.

The route for Method Man's romantic move had been paved in 1987 by the rapper, L L Cool J's song, "I Need Love." The rapper claims that changing his name from James Todd Smith to Ladies Love Cool J, was an adolescent wish come true. Despite the beatings he received from his stepfather, L L knew what it was to receive family love and help. Muscles shifting beneath his cut-off T-shirt, the rapper recalled in 1991, "It started when I was nine years old in the early '80s, a wave of rap records and tapes circulating throughout the community: the Cold Crush Brothers, the Fantastic Romantic Freaks. I didn't go to too many parties because I was young, but I used to tell my grandmother what records I wanted and she'd go to the record store and she'd bring them back and I'd listen." He smiles nostalgically. "It was like rap school."[23]

Just as Bill Withers decribed in "Grandma's Hands," L L's grandmother's love helped give him the stability he needed to break through.

It takes a lot of grit to stick with it when life or the industry knocks you back, and some artists' egos need more feeding than they get. Phyllis Hyman had scored a Tony nomination for the stage show *Sophisticated Ladies* as well as acclaim for such albums as *Goddess of Love* and *Living All Alone*. But not even the prospect of making a new record with the noted Philadelphia Sound producers Kenny Gamble and Leon Huff helped Hyman feel she loved life enough to stick around.

Many in the music industry believe depression, insecurity, and illness made the singer cancel her starring role in a musical. In an industry obsessed with slim women, she may have been devastated that her weight had soared. Days before her forty-sixth birthday, Hyman overdosed on sleeping pills, leaving behind a note that said, "I'm tired. I'm tired."[24]

Issues of body image led singer Martha Wash to court. Wash was formerly part of the effervescent Two Tons of Fun, a backup group for drag disco-diva Sylvester. She and her singing partner went on to sing as the Weather Girls. Wash supplied the lung power for dance hits like Black Box's "Everybody, Everybody," and C & C Music Factory's "Gonna Make You Sweat." When Wash was replaced by a slender woman in the videos for the song, she sued for fraud.

It takes a focused woman to overcome such obstacles, but looks weren't the only thing standing in the way of female artists. As Ronnie Spector discovered, being an adjunct of a powerful producer is a restricted-access ticket liable to be withdrawn if the relationship cracks. Spector was the wife and Pygmalion protégé of producer Phil Spector. Phil, the Wall of Sound wunderkind, produced "River Deep, Moutain High," with Ike and Tina Turner. Phil made Ronnie the heroine of epic mini-operas like "Leader of the Pack," with her trio, the Ronettes. A vixen in bouffant hair and stiletto heels, who loved bad biker boys, Ronnie's image and the throb in her voice were not forgotten after she split from her influential husband. But it was rough for her to rebuild a career, solo.

Tina Turner also rebuilt her career after a conflict-infected relationship. She had the loudest last laugh. So flash that she taught young Mick Jagger his moves, nonetheless, Tina was under the thumb of her abusive husband, the bandleader Ike Turner. Finding the guts to split and tell all in print and on screen made Tina a near-saintly figure. In that progression, her music changed from the Southern R&B, whose howl she'd owned, to a smooth, rock-based stadium sound.

However, the careers of many great singers never hit the sustain button. Though her talent was never in doubt, Motown's Brenda Holloway had little chart success as an artist apart from 1964's "Every Little Bit Hurts," a cut so intense that she received an R&B Foundation Pioneers Award in 1998. Holloway sang with Barry White on his album *Staying Power* in the late 1990s. In the intervening years, her torch was kept aflame by Britain's 1970s Northern Soul movement. Enthusiasts traded obscure vinyl for sums greater than the artists ever earned, and championed forgotten artists at amphetamine-fueled, marathon all-nighters.

These all-nighters mirror those at gay clubs, long the laboratories of dance music. Guitarist and producer Nile Rodgers, co-founder of the disco-era band, Chic, remembers, "The gay clubs were where you really heard innovative disco dance music. They had the best sound systems and the best opticals. At Studio 54, if you didn't look like you belonged, they wouldn't let you in. But the gay clubs didn't have to answer to anyone; they were already operating on the outside, the fringe. They had their own economic power, their own rules."

"I started to go to gay clubs to see if I

Phyllis Hyman London 1987

Evelyn "Champagne" King London 1985

Natalie Cole London 1987

Gwen Guthrie London 1983

Jocelyn Brown London 1992

Clockwise from top left: Millie Jackson London 1984, Ronnie Spector London 1980, Chaka Khan London 1985, Mary J. Blige New Jersey 1995

## Tina Turner

London 1983

could learn something from what they had happening, their rebellious, underground, almost left-wing attitude," Rodgers continued. "I noticed a lot of female impersonators, who would come not just in drag, but in costume. It was like Halloween every night. They were the precursors of the club kids. There was always a Diana Ross, a Judy Garland, or a Barbra Streisand. I realized that they loved these divas, these women who were larger than life."

One such diva is the exuberant Chaka Khan. She is cited as an inspiration by younger singers such as Mary J. Blige and Monica. Khan's majestic voice out-funked her original band, Rufus. Solo, she recorded the dramatic, "Ain't Nobody," the surging "I Feel For You," and the epic, "I'm Every Woman."

Despite Khan's presence, by its very nature, much club music is faceless. The real stars are the dancers. But there are divas whose individuality comes through, even when they're indelibly associated with one particular track, such as Gwen Guthrie's caustic "Ain't Nothing Goin' On But the Rent," Evelyn "Champagne" King's "Shame," and Jocelyn Brown's exhilarating song of disillusionment, "Somebody Else's Guy."

In the British club scene of the 1980s, multiracial groups, like the flamboyantly dressed Culture Club, blurred the boundaries between genders and music genres like reggae and R&B. Looks and style sometimes seemed as important as musical ability. In fashionable nightclubs like the Wag, the understated style and sensuality of Nigerian-born fashion student Sade Adu immediately attracted attention. Approving first glances were reinforced by her silky style of Brazilian bossa-nova meets jazz vocals on "Smooth Operator," with the band Pride. Sade developed into a cool, sophisticated solo artist exuding class and refined romance.

While music all around her pumped through the speakers, Sade dropped the volume, and her whisper proved as powerful as dance music's hectic beats per minute.

The Jamaican producer, Coxsone Dodd, recalls a parallel moment when the urgency of 1960s ska music—the sound of Jamaica's heady independence—slowed down into rock steady. "The people just got tired of dancing so fast. It was time to slow down the beat," Dodd said.

Gentle seduction was applied by "Mr. Rock Steady," the debonair Alton Ellis, sometimes in

Sadé London 1986

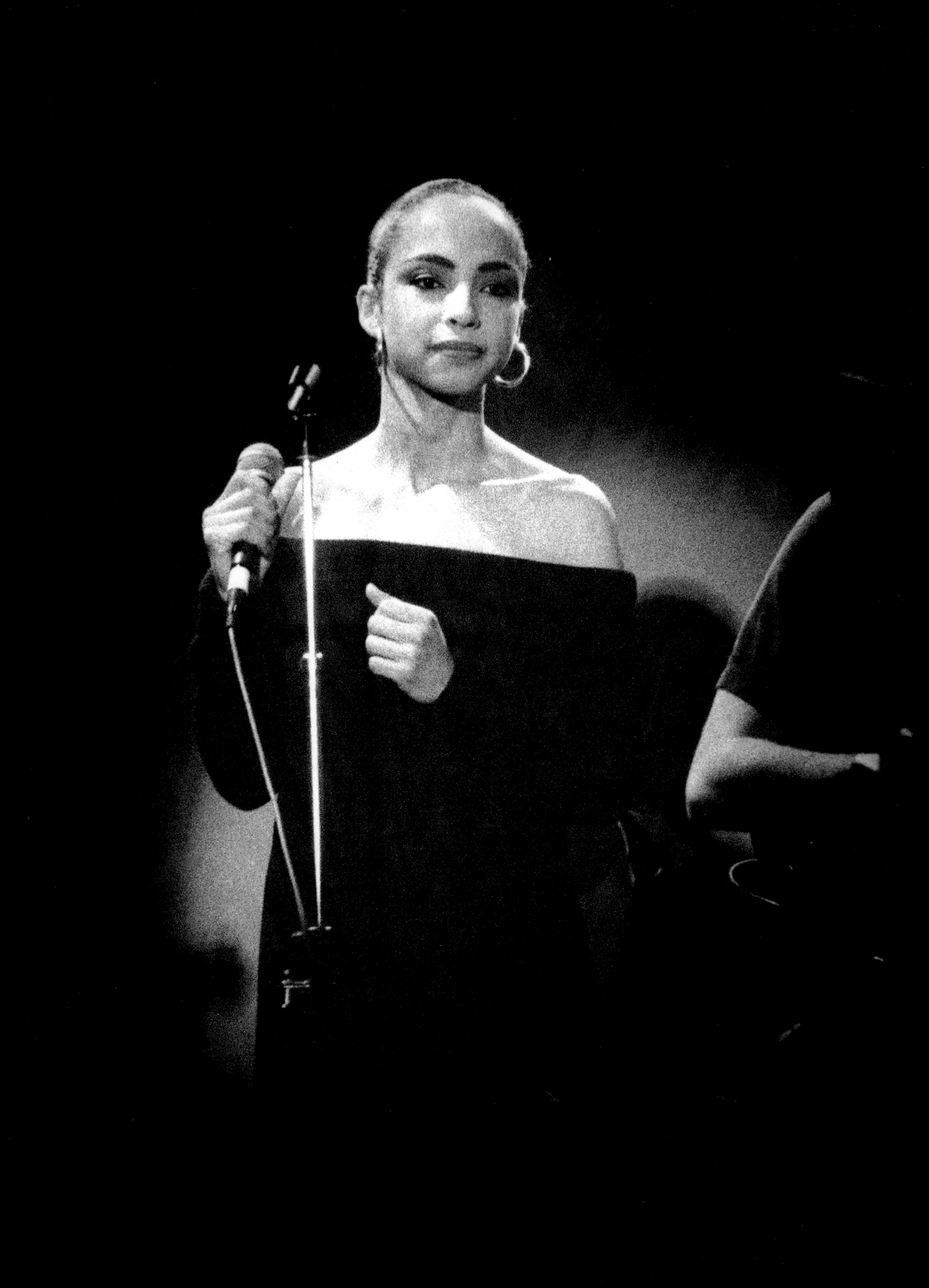

Brenda Holloway London 1987

# Dionne Warwick
London 1982

81

Alton Ellis London 1984

company with his sister, Hortense.

A romantic, non-macho lover, Ellis challenged the swaggering "rude boys" on tracks like "Cry Tough," asking, "How can a man be tough, tougher than the world?"

The unaffected velvet voice of John Holt, lead singer of the Paragons trio, also defined rock steady imploring on tracks like "(I'm Gonna) Wear You to the Ball Tonight" and "The Tide Is High." Most reggae artists were chasing crossover dreams in the early 1970s. The magic love potion was mixed by Holt with his album "One Thousand Volts of Holt," an intergenerational, Saturday-night-grind staple.

The digital sound of dancehall shifted Jamaican pop from Holt's "rubadub" slow-dance style and earthy reggae drum and bass, to chattering, severe strokes of synthesized drums in the years following Bob Marley's death in 1981.

The rugged ghetto youth, Shabba Ranks, publicized his healthy sexual appetite in 1980s tracks like "Wicked In Bed" and "Trailer Loads of Girls." Shabba's sometimes ironic swagger and bravado, imposing physical presence, and gritty growl endeared him to American rappers. In his duet with British singer Maxi Priest, "Mr. Loverman," his rough voice contrasted exquisitely with Priest's sweet tone.

Another Jamaican singer, Buju Banton, provoked outrage with his odes to love. His song to light-skinned girls "Mi Love Mi Brownin," provoked such a negative response that he immediately cut a song in response, "Love Black Woman." That commmotion was overshadowed by the controversy that was provoked when the patois of the teenager's 1992 single, "Boom Bye Bye," was deciphered outside Jamaica as an incitement to kill homosexuals.

Banton's defenders claimed that the song was just theatrical rhetoric or that it expressed the feelings of the Jamaican majority along with many others' songs. Nevertheless, homosexual persecution is an issue in Jamaica. The song prompted an international campaign that effectively stalled Banton's career, also effecting Shabba Ranks, who, in defending his friend, had made antihomosexual comments on live British TV. Defiantly, Banton struck a blow for his moral character by casting himself as a prophet of the people on a fiery reggae album, *Till Shiloh*. The music featured the Rasta "grounation" drums as a touchstone of integrity.

Soon after came the breakthrough of New Jack Swing in America, which encouraged new voices of love in Jamaica such as Beres Hammond and Beenie Man.

Unlike Ranks and Banton, Beenie Man (a pet name for a small child)sings tunefully and developed the "sing-jay" style that mixes singing with DJ'ing. His authoritative voice and high-speed technique flow seamlessly through R&B, rap, and reggae. His gift for mimic and his quick wits have sustained a career that began at eight years old. As a former child star whose adult career blossomed, Beenie Man belongs to a tradition that includes Freddie McGregor and Dennis Brown, whose sweet voices introduced the romantic style called Lover's Rock.

Over modern, sparse productions by Donovan Germain, the late-night intimacy of Beres Hammond's voice reinterprets John Holt's, "Love I Can Feel," and "Tempted To Touch." Though Hammond's voice is less delicate, his deft phrasing is an uncanny echo of another Jamaican heartthrob singer, Gregory Isaacs.

Lean and debonair in a high-crowned hat and sharp white suit Gregory Isaacs is "The Cool Ruler." Smooth seductions like his 1982 track, "Night Nurse," in which he stars as the "patient by the name of Gregory," combine with his languid, ladykiller grin to make him good gigolo material. Isaacs' balancing act between the caress of his voice and his outlaw confrontations with the police make him a living amalgam of Don and Don Juan.

The original "Gangster of Love" was written by Johnny "Guitar" Watson, a guitar wizard with a suggestive voice. The Los Angeles blues player who inspired the young Jimi Hendrix by playing the guitar backwards and upside down recalled the days when he was one of the so-called Magnificent Seven—seven guys with seven Cadillacs and seven girls each. "Yeah, we were players," he chuckled nostalgically. "We were just hip guys in the streets. The Mack look is glamorous. All the young guys want to be players, have lots of women, money, flash cars, and jewelry. We were the fathers of these images. I guess the times have finally caught up with me."[26]

Following the Gangster of Love's lead came Brooklyn rapper, the Notorious B.I.G. or Biggie Smalls. A former crack dealer, he was an unconventional sex symbol, given a resemblance to the portly Alfred Hitchcock that Biggie himself liked to riff on. "Biggie had the charm. He was a very sweet person. He was like the Mack!" remembers rapper Missy Elliott, smiling. Biggie was among those rappers whose objectification of women into bitches and ho's influenced artists

Kingston, Jamaica 1993 — Buju Banton

New York 1995 (left) — Beenie Man

London 1986 (right) — Freddie McGregor

Gregory Isaacs London 1984 (right)

Shabba Ranks London 1990 (left)

Beres Hammond Kingston, Jamaica 1993

London 1986 L.L. Cool J

Salt N'Pepa

New York 1994

87

**New York 1998**

# Missy Elliott

like rappers L'il Kim and Foxy Brown to be "bitches" and proud.

"We're both saying the same thing, but L'il Kim is straight to the point," observes Missy Elliott. "She's taking the bedroom to the radio, speaking out on what a lot of people say."

Having been involved in gangs as a teenager, Barry White is well-versed in ghetto love. "You know, no matter what they say about gangster rappers, they still tell the truth, honey. When you hear them talking about ho's and bitches and 'I want to do this to you,' that's where they come from."

The gynecological goddesses of the late 1990s, like Foxy Brown, can trace their heritage back to Millie Jackson. A shocker for her time—the pre-AIDS 1970s-Jackson was a big mouth whose free-talking ways earned her a reputation as the queen of sleaze.

"As a woman, she could speak her mind, have pride of self, and express herself," commented her former singing partner, Isaac Hayes. "If she was in love or wanted a man, she said it. If she didn't want to be bothered, she said that, too. It was a kind of freedom."

Just as boastful about her physical abilities and needs as Jackson or Ranks, Jamaica's Lady Saw put out a call for a "hard-working man" as her bedfellow, in the 1990s. Her "batty-rider" micro-mini shorts drew attention to her shrewd musical observation that true obscenity is not found in a song, but in corrupt politicians.

All bold reggae and rap femmes were begat by the fishnet-clad loins of original girl rappers Salt'n'Pepa. Their lyrics "Push it real good!" and "Let's talk about sex" announced needs that could have come from phone-booth sex advertisements.

The videos for "What A Man" and "Shoop" showed Salt'n'Pepa draped in adoring hunks. Flaunting leather any dominatrix would pay to order, rappers Salt'n'Pepa were on the video set of "Ain't Nuthin' But A She Thing," raising money for women's health in 1996. "I'm glad that this group showed we could be female rappers and still be female," said Salt, aka Cheryl James. "There's nothing wrong with being sexy as long as you can show someone that you're intelligent, you have a brain, and demand your respect."[27] Cracking the whip in her shiny black gloved hand, she licked her lips and vamped to the camera.

"We're always gonna be sexy, I don't care what you say!" added Sandy "Pepa" Denton. "We're gonna show it all!"[28]

In her combination of reckless bravado, worldiness, and pain—gift-wrapped in haute couture—Mary J. Blige became the 1990s "Queen of

Soul." Her songs suggest a haughty veneer, which hides the vulnerability within. She's hardened herself for the sort of separation she experienced with her initial producer/Svengali, Sean "Puffy" Combs.

"Well it kind of hurt that I had to leave," Blige recalled. "It hurt one day and it hurt the next day, but it hurt a little bit less the more that I went out there on my own. And now it doesn't hurt anymore at all."[29]

Traveling on the road with the band Jodeci, Blige had the opportunity to see lust at its most rampant, exhibited by the band's female followers. "The women, they're just out screaming, hollering, chasing (the band). Oh, my God, it was sickening. Male groupies, they'll look and they'll just keep looking."[30]

But looking for fulfillment in a fantasy may seem safer than risking a real relationship, as Missy Elliott understands.

"People don't talk about love on the hip-hop side, they're more into an expression of what's going on around them in their neighborhood every day. A lot of trust in relationships is not there any more, as opposed to back in the day. People think, "I'm not gonna fall in love and put this burden on my heart."

Love veteran Barry White has his own philosophy. "The signs of love, they're never gonna change. There are women and men in the world who are very happy in love. There are more women and men who are not happy in love. Some people will hear a song when they're in love, and love love itself. Some people who break up from their relationships don't wanna hear nothing about love. It just depends on what mood you're in. But there's definitely something healing about a love song, baby."

Notorious B.I.G. New Jersey 1996

Johnny "Guitar" Watson — London 1987

Method Man (Wu Tang Clan) New York 1995

Following page: Jodeci Fans New Jersey 1996

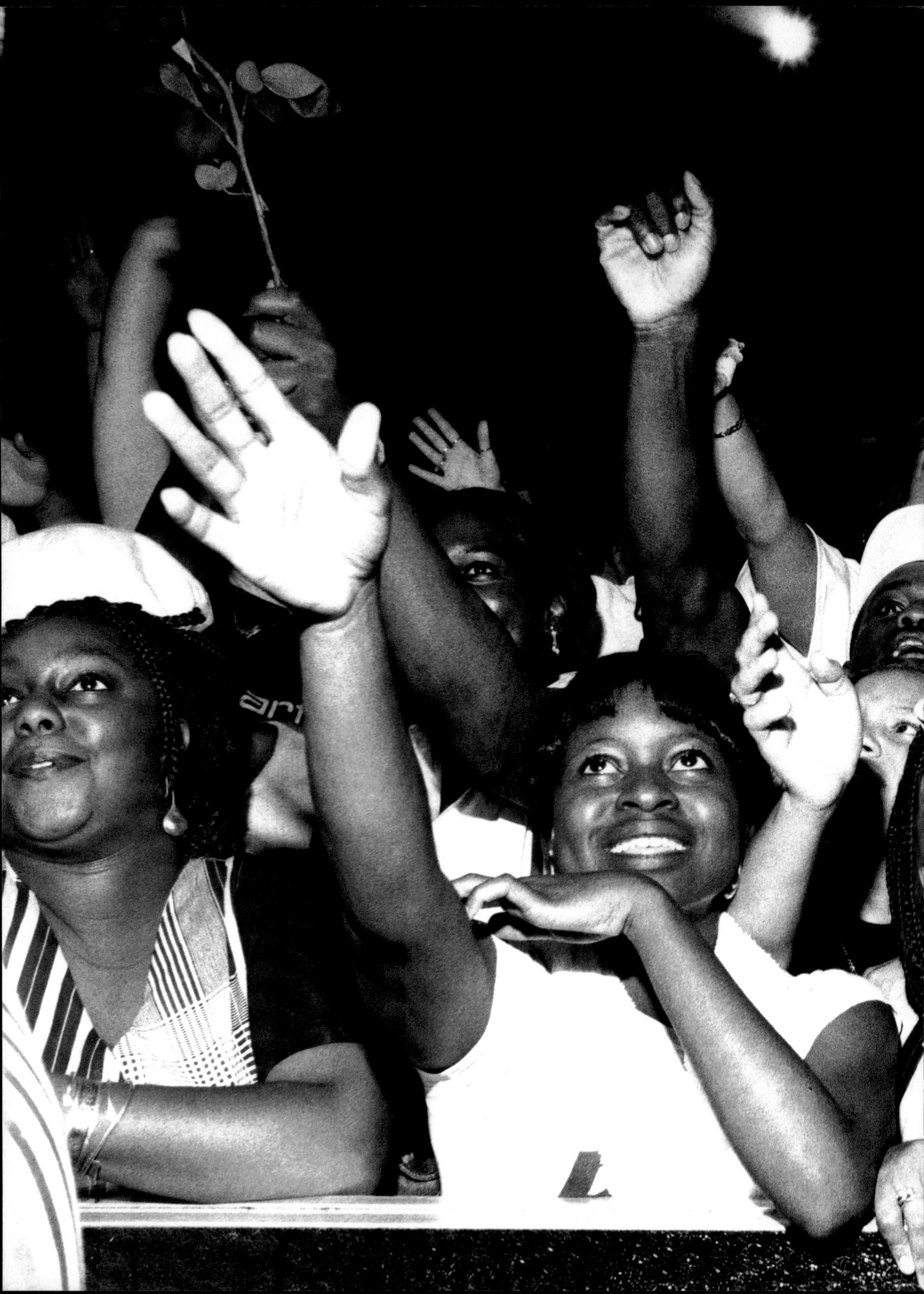

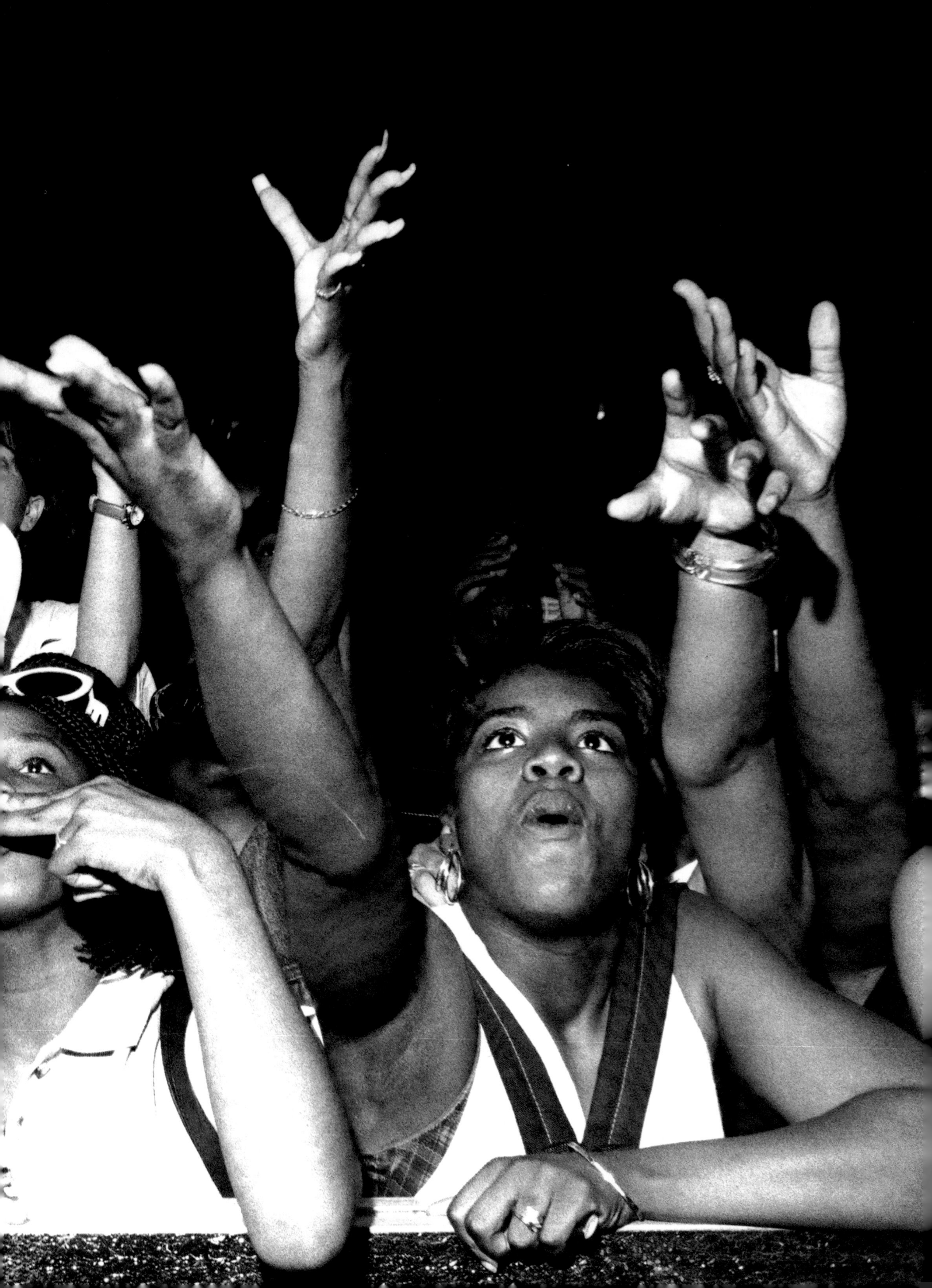

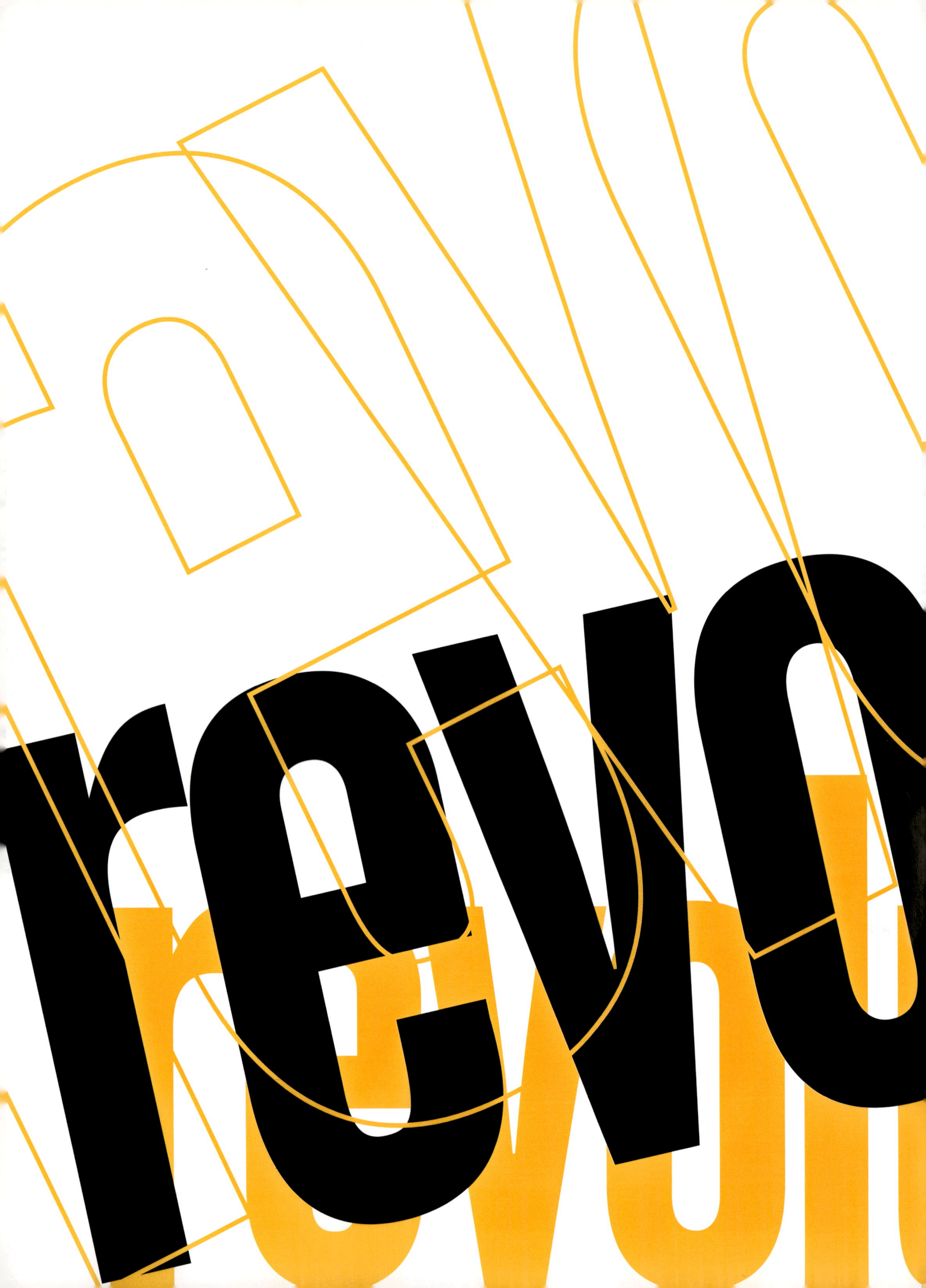
revo

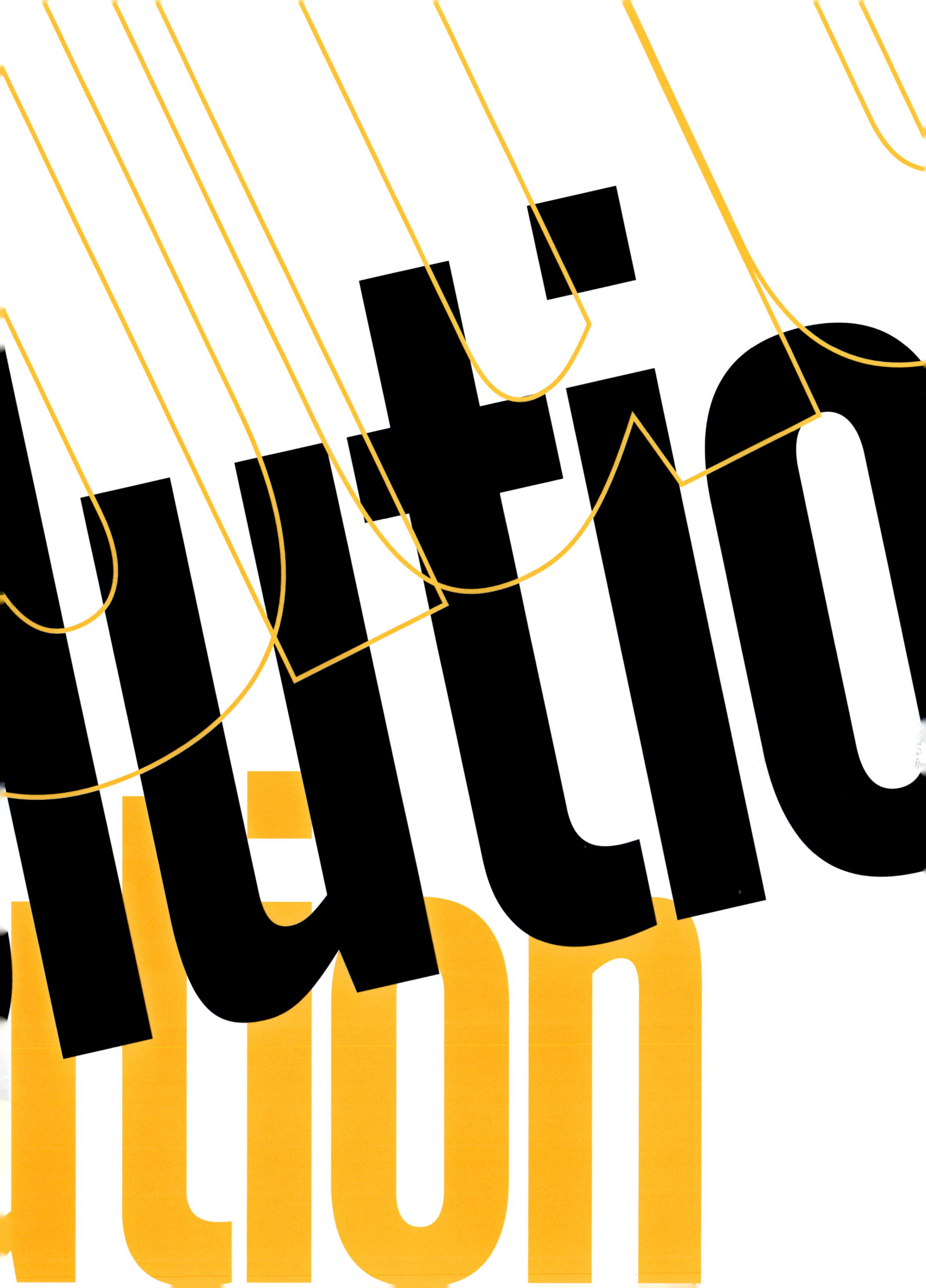
lutio
tion

London 1983.
Fela Kuti

# Revolution

"Every man have him work fe do," Bob Marley liked to say. Man or woman, revolutionary musicians fight along with their songs, but involvement in actual "shoot-out" action is not essential for effective action. American poet/performer Gil Scott-Heron's funky "The Revolution Will Not Be Televised" was a creative, non-violent message that potently reminded people that they were in control. Rap group Public Enemy's apocalyptic denunciations of the American way mobilized political awareness among the global hip-hop generation—their only arrests were for Flavor Flav's gun and drug possessions rather than for their rhetoric.

But for artists on the front line in developing countries—artists such as Nigeria's Fela Anikulapo-Kuti; Jamaica's Bob Marley; and South African People's Poet Mzwakhe Mbuli—jail, torture, and, often, an early death have been the results of being politically outspoken and active. Their salvation is that they have all helped propel the change that they sang about.

"In every political movement there's always a cultural movement that runs in tandem. One complements the other, one is not a substitute for the other," clarified Linton Kwesi Johnson. Johnson, the original dub poet, stopped making music for some years to fulfill his obligations to Race Today, his political-collective organization in London's Brixton neighborhood.

Progress can be brought about even by a comparatively apolitical artist like Michael Jackson, a child star with his family group, the Jackson Five. The adorable Motown wunderkind was all about upbeat, uncomplicated fun. As an adult, Jackson has recorded some humanistic songs with Quincy Jones, like "The Man In The Mirror," to balance his shiny dance confections.

But Jackson ultimately overcame his usual reticence and hit MTV hard in the early 1980s, when he refused to let his much awaited videos be played unless MTV changed their practice of only playing videos by white artists. Jackson's surreal and innovative videos were a potent card to play, and MTV agreed his demands. Jackson had broken MTV's color barrier.

On a more overtly political bent, many talents contributed to the Civil Rights Movement. The cultural aspects of Martin Luther King Jr.'s organization were arranged by the Student Non-Violent Coordinating Committee, or SNCC. Groups included the Freedom Singers and Stokely Carmichael's (later Kwame Toure) Harambe Singers. Both choirs were organized by Bernice Johnson Reagan, who went on to cofound the socially conscious a cappella group Sweet Honey in the Rock.

The folk singer Odetta, like her peers Bob Dylan and Rambling Jack McGee, always performed solo. "Alone with her guitar, she was called to speak out and sing her folk, blues, and spirituals at all the political and cultural rallies," recalls singer Jayne Cortez. "The songs she sang came out of the movement that started when we left Africa and continued with Paul Robeson, Miriam Makeba, and others. Odetta's one of the strong voices."

Also traveling a difficult road alone was another SNCC regular—the intense pianist and singer Nina Simone. She lobbed musical hand grenades with her deep, husky delivery on "Mississipi Goddam," her eulogy for the slain Civil Rights leader Medgar Evers, and again years later, with the wrenching Randy Newman composition, "Baltimore, Ain't it Hard Just to Live," a lament for one of America's worst killing fields of young Black males.

Exposure to the suffering of Black South Africans under the apartheid system, which kept the country's original inhabitants in serfdom and completely segregated them from the white ruling class, broadened the awareness of a global Black struggle. As Maya Angelou writes in her memoir, *Heart of A Woman*, "Harry Belafonte...was working with a South African singer, Miriam Makeba, and South Africa was really no different than South Philly."[31] In some ways, the greater struggle was endured by musicians like sax player Kippie Moketsi, who stayed behind in South Africa, but the township refugees who arrived in America from South Africa in the 1950s, played a crucial role.

The lively urban center Sophiatown, where Zulu and Sotho artists were collaborating and breaking boundaries, was bulldozed. The government used tribalism to try and smash the vibrant Black culture. They forcibly moved Sophiatown residents to bleak new townships like Soweto that were divided according to tribe. With one blow, the South African big-band jazz scene was gutted. The scene revived in the 1960s with the very different sound of small electric bands playing the Zulu backbeat of *mbaqanga* music.

The all-African jazz opera *King Kong*, which opened in 1959, was pivotal to the spread of South African culture. That a musical with a Black cast was not only staged but also permitted to travel abroad was unique in the country's history. South Africa's artistic elite was showcased in the production, which included the harmony group the Manhattan Brothers (a favorite of Nelson Mandela, leader of the African National Congress [ANC]); singer-songwriter Caiphus Semenya; his wife, singer Letta M'bulu; Jonas Gwangwa. Hugh Masekela was the musical director. Many of the cast defected from South Africa while on the tour and sought political asylum in London and Sweden, invigorating the music of their new hometowns.

"Apartheid was really in. I said, 'Jesus, I gotta get out of here,'" remembers Masekela. "I got my passport in 1960, right after the Sharpeville Massacre (in which schoolchildren protesting the enforced use of identity pass cards were killed by the army). I was in the Jazz Disciples with Kippy; we were the first Black group to have an LP out. Then, all gatherings of more than ten people were banned, so we cancelled our tour."[32]

Marrying Stokeley Carmichael, who later joined the Black Panther party, meant that Miriam Makeba's music would be effectively banned in America. But when she first arrived, as Masekela said, "She threw the place wide open with Dizzy Gillespie."[33]

Many of South Africa's gifted female vocalists such as Dorothy Masuka, Dolly Rathebe, and the female harmony group The Dark City Sisters, often worked in the American jazz or doo-wop styles. Prominent among them was the golden voice of Makeba along with her fellow singers in the Skylarks trio, Johanna Radebe and Mary Robotapi.

Makeba was among the first Black South African artists allowed to travel abroad. Makeba remembered, "I met Harry Belafonte in London, and he was very influential in getting me an American visa. Two years after I left, *King Kong* came to England and Belafonte arranged for Hugh [Masekela] to get into the Manhattan School of Music."[34]

"A lot of people had great faith in him,"[35] explained Belafonte. Among them was Dizzy Gillespie, who was pioneering Cu-bop, the blend of Afro-Cuba and bebop jazz. He embraced the opportunity to work with Hugh. "The Africans had a good sense of going back to the beginning of the music."

Quincy Jones elaborated, "Hugh came from another direction. Dizzy took American music and fused it with African drums, and Hugh did it the other way 'round."

Masekela effected a remarkable penetration of American culture, jamming with jazz musicians such as the Crusaders and West Coast hippy musicians such as the Byrds, as well as scoring a number-one single, "Grazing in the Grass," in the mid-1960s. But he never forgot his introduction to the city of his dreams, New York.

"I knew where to go in town as soon as I arrived," Masekela enthused nostalgically. On his first night in Manhattan, he caught John Coltrane, Miles Davis, Monk and Dizzy, Mingus, Count Basie with Sarah Vaughan, Horace Silver with Machito, and Tito Puente. "I ended up at a 3 A.M. show, catching Abbey Lincoln. I was in my world. I couldn't wait to write home the next day."[36]

Singing in a clinging red gown once sported by Marilyn Monroe, Lincoln became famous for her cameo in the 1950s movie *The Girl Can't Help It*. Hers was the husky voice on (her then husband) Max Roach's *Freedom Now Suite*, slashing at the apartheid regime with tracks like "Driver Man." Maya Angelou recalled, "The Max Roach/Abbey Lincoln records were smuggled into South Africa and then passed around like the hot revolutionary material they were."[37]

"That was not my music," clarified Lincoln. "I was the voice on it. But if you go on your

Dennis Brown
London 1984

# Michael

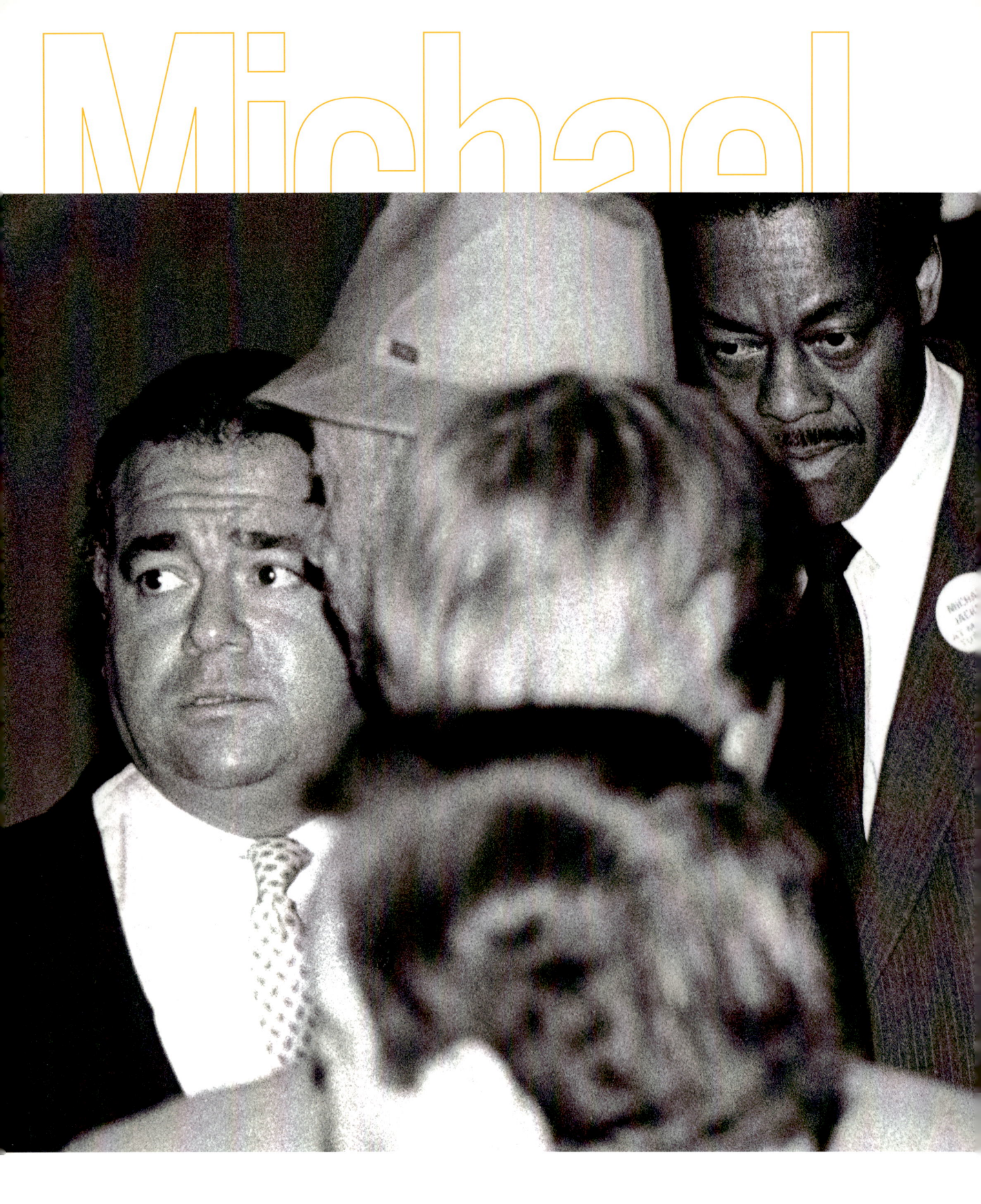

10⁰

Jackson

London 1985

New York 1994

# Aretha Franklin

own and try to make a contribution, you have to pay dues, and I paid mine. After I recorded *Straight Ahead* and the *Freedom Now Suite*, I was not invited to record in America again for many years. But I was in three films, including *The Girl Can't Help It*. I wrote poems and a play and I painted. I practice the arts. I don't put my career first, it's the work. And if your work is good you'll have a career."

On her return to recording in the early 1990s, she immediately topped the *Billboard* magazine jazz charts with "You Gotta Pay The Band" and has continued to record contemplative, uplifting music, like her song of zen detachment, "Throw It Away" that bears out her philosophy: "People who practice music and the arts should be just a little higher in the house to help illuminate things."

Aretha Franklin's place in the house is the Amen Corner, where the finest church singers wail. She brought gospel fervor to her consistent endorsement of Martin Luther King, Jr., who was a familiar guest at the house of her father, the Reverend C.L. Franklin. When she was offered the keys to her hometown, Detroit, it was King who handed them to her. At King's funeral in April 1968, as she had often done at his request, Aretha sang the Rev. Thomas Dorsey's moving hymn "Precious Lord."

Protesting King's assassination, rioters sent Boston up in flames. Though militants criticized him as a reactionary, it was James Brown who gave some peace to the people with a live performance at the Boston Garden. With individualistic patriotism, Brown supported a series of the nation's leaders, dubbing Gerald Ford the "Funky President" in 1974. But his central contribution was shouting out what could previously only be whispered in anthems like "Say It Loud, I'm Black and I'm Proud!" in 1968. The timing of Brown's releases branded them indelibly on the era's momentous events. Brown recorded his declaration of change, "Papa's Got A Brand New Bag," in the month of Malcolm X's assassination. Three weeks after its release, rioters torched the Watts neighborhood in Los Angeles in reaction to Malcolm X's death.

In the segregated Depression-era South, where Brown was raised, a dark-skinned orphan like Brown was automatically a member of the

Nina Simone London 1984

Odetta London 1981

Hugh Masekela New York 1998

Fugees — New York 1994

Miriam Makeba — London 1988

underclass. Perhaps because of frustration from living in such a society, Brown had early problems with the law. He served a hard-labor sentence for breaking into four cars in one night, but discipline and heavenly talents eventually turned him into the Godfather of Soul and the Hardest Working Man in Show Business. He rewrote the rules.

The James Brown band, the JB's, was a talent pool that featured saxophonist Maceo Parker and Fred Wesley. Given the sexual force of his "licking-stick" music, perhaps it's no surprise that many of the King's "Queens"—the women in the James Brown organization such as Lynn Collins and Marvelous Marva Whitney, as well as Marvin Gaye's future singing partner Tammi Terrell—were romantically involved with their boss. It was a dubious career move, as many left the group in the painful relationship aftermaths.

Vicki Anderson was one of the few Queens who did not get involved with Brown. "Shortly after I joined the show, I met, fell in love with, and married Bobby Byrd. That took a lot of stress off me,"[38] she laughed.

But those stormy relationships were also fruitful. Lyn Collins recalled that "(Brown) said, 'Okay, Lyn, this is the time of Women's Lib so I think it's time for you to do a song.'"[39] The result, a stirring challenge called "Think About It," was given another, sampled life in the Rob Base hit "It Takes Two."

Proving the staying power of the collaborations between the King and his Queens, L'il Kim sampled the track "Message from the Soul Sisters."

As previously stated in Heart and Soul, Curtis Mayfield had lived the downside of the American Dream. Luring listeners into activism with heavenly harmonies in the months before the 1964 Civil Rights Act passed, Mayfield's gently persistent encouragement in "Keep On Pushing" became a hit on all the American charts. The message was equally explicit in a 1968 recording: "This is my country, I paid three hundred years or more of slave-driving sweat and welts on my back...." That same year, the assertive affirmation "We're A Winner" was powerful enough to be virtually banned from radio—and yet it hit the charts as both a pop and R&B hit.

A surge of forceful voices articulated the change in the political cry from Civil Rights to Black Power in the 1960s. Soulful Nina Simone sang her catchy mantra "Young, Gifted and Black" in 1969. Within the year it was covered by a young Jamaican duo, the thoughtful Bob Andy and Marcia Griffiths, who later sang behind Bob Marley in the I-Three trio. In reggae mode, Simone's message became an international hit.

Also in the 1970s, Marvin Gaye defied Detroit's Motown—the temple of American Black pop—by refusing to be confined to crooning. "I think it was around 1969 or 1970 when I stopped thinking so much about my erotic fantasies and started thinking about the war in Vietnam. My brother used to tell me...some pretty horrible stories about the war,"[40] he recalled quietly. Gaye's response to Vietnam, "What's Going On," was a plaintive plea for the world. His boss, Motown founder Berry Gordy, didn't want to release the breakthrough disc, and later justified his decision. "I had a reputation for good, solid music, I didn't want to put a protest album out on my label."[41] The album was shelved for more than a year until Gordy finally agreed to its release. The album's overwhelming international reception proved that Gaye was not alone in questioning the old approaches and seeking new ones.

Responding to the same urge for honesty and a new beginning, Motown's Temptations were also transforming from classy but conventional church-based vocalists to psychedelic social commentators, guided by producer Norman Whitfield.

The progressive atmosphere also inspired Motown's child phenomenon "Little" Stevie Wonder, the blind piano and harmonica player. Paralleling Gaye's bid for business and creative independence, Wonder matured on landmark albums, such as *Talking Book* and *Innervisions*, which had a new awareness and were peppered with post-Watergate paranoia. "We, as Americans, are moving in the right direction and we can recognize those who, like King, gave their lives for the principles of our country. [It is] the only way for the United States to stay united people of the states," Wonder said at a 1983 press conference celebrating the institution of Martin Luther King, Jr. Day.

Freedom of expression became a need that nudged Curtis Mayfield away from his longtime fellow harmonizers, the Impressions. "I was writing songs that were quite difficult for the other four Impressions to comprehend during the early stages of my creativity,"[42] he chuckled. A more urgent sound marked his first solo album, the volcanic *Curtis*, with its profound "(We People) Who Are Darker Than Blue" and spacey neo-dub effects on "(Don't Worry) If There's a Hell Below, We're All Going To Go."

Different times find different messengers. The griot role of witness was eagerly seized in the 1990s by rapper-group Public Enemy. Formed in Long Island (known in the hip-hop community as "Strong Island") University's campus radio station, Chuck D shared Brown's ability to name the moment. He influenced attitudes and events with titles such as, "It Takes A Nation Of Millions to Hold Us Back." His polemic was reinforced by his volatile sidekick Flavor Flav, whose comical, disjointed patter disguised some savage truths. The volume on their message was turned up by the dramatic soundscapes of their producer, Hank Shocklee. Their music cut through the regular club fare like a screaming siren.

"I travel all over the country, I go to jails, I talk to the brothers. They feel just as if they were still at the bottom of the slaves ship, lying there with their sisters, sleeping in their own [mess]. It's not me or Ice Cube or [rapper/activist Sister] Souljah's feelings—we're just the messengers, and how you gonna kill the messengers?

"When we started out, [political rap] was not in vogue. The black male image in the mid-'80s was Prince or Michael Jackson and you were not really defiant. If you was, you was wearing a gold rope and you were a hoodlum. The Los Angeles riots—or rebellion—of 1992 made people look differently at that Black man or woman."[43]

The Los Angeles uprising in areas such as Compton, Watts, and South Central grounded the raps of Ice Cube and Ice T in reality.

Neneh Cherry spent some of her teenage years in Compton with her grandmother in the 1970s. "When I went back after a few years, a lot of the kids I socialized with were dead or in jail. The percentage of young Black men who don't make it to twenty-five or get locked up is huge. It's a real struggle. The rappers are talking about something real."

When his career was established, Ice T moved from Compton to Hollywood Hills, to whose usual inhabitants "South Central could be Vietnam or that far away."[44] Many of the Compton streets on which Ice T was raised, with their neat houses and lawns, looked prettily suburban. But as he said, they were still "the killing fields," where the rival gangs, including the notorious Crips and Bloods, fight their wars.

The media furor over Ice T's track "Cop Killer," from his heavy metal album *Body Count*, brought Ice T national notoriety and became a landmark in America's censorship battles. Records deemed offensive were ordered to display a warning sticker. Ice-T commented on the sticker in the song "Freedom of Speech." "You gotta be high to believe, you can change the world with a sticker on a record sleeve."

The street hustling glorified in gangsta rap has been dubbed "bloody capitalism" by Biggie's friend, writer Dream Hampton. Employment has to be lucrative to lure some successful gangstas from the underworld existence known as "The Life." "When I stopped hustling and started making songs, it was the worst. My advance from Bad Boy was just petty money, like 12, 20 G's,"[45] said Biggie to *Vibe* magazine in 1995. It was a far cry from the "money money" the big man was used to scoring from selling crack.

Missy Elliott, the first young Black female artist to be given her own record label by a multinational parent company, is in touch with currents in the rap community. She commented about Biggie Smalls, "One thing about Biggie is that he lived the life he talked about, you got to respect that. He grew up around drugs," she said. "We can't ignore that people do wake up and see other people getting shot, crackheads on their corner, and sell drugs because they've got to feed their kids. A lot of rap songs have become about materialism."

Some say the thug life caught up with rappers Tupac Shakur and Biggie Smalls. Both died from fatal gunshot wounds, and suspects in both cases have been linked to gangs. Twenty-five years after Mayfield recorded "Freddy's Dead," a lament for a fallen hustler from his 1972 *Superfly* soundtrack, the singer softly quoted the lines from the song upon hearing of Shakur's death: "He never knew that his hope was a rope." Mayfield added, "I really think that maybe [he] played that gang image too hot or too hard. Deep inside, Tupac was probably a nicer guy than we will ever know, but his image in the movies was that he was always a bad, mean kid. I would say he might have become caught up into that and the things he might say or do in his rap became personalized among him and other people who just didn't like it. It brought him down before his time."[46]

Although gangsta rap was an honest representation of some aspects of ghetto reality, its cold-blooded attitude could not define hip hop. In reaction, a new musical and lyrical balance was struck by a generation for whom sampling was as natural as strumming a guitar. Once again, the idea of authenticity became a touchstone of integrity, and in the 1990s that meant "old school." Within hip-hop, the term referred to rap's 1970's originators, like Doug E. Fresh, Afrika Bambaataa, and Run DMC. Broadly, old school identified the most moving elements of soul: empassioned gospel vocalizing, a tight

**Abbey Lincoln** New York 1998

rhythm section, a full-blown horn section, and emotional honesty.

The Fugees—short for "refugees"—have injected old school into latter-day hip-hop, with their name triggering associations with the struggles of Haitian immigrant families and displaced people everywhere. Lauryn Hill, Wyclef Jean, and Prakazrel "Pras" Duplessi—New Jersey school friends—played hip-hop on instruments and projected ghetto survivalism steeped in a sense of morality. It was a process extended by Hill on her first solo album, *The Miseducation of Lauryn Hill*. Following their example, a pre-millennial, socially conscious generation arose. Their priestesses were singers such as Hill and Erykah Badu; Outkast (produced by Babyface) and Philadelphia's the Roots.

Socially conscious rap balanced gangster style, but rap still illustrated certain conflicts that were not necessarily deadly ones. "Snapping," a game of trading insults as entertainment, was practiced during the era of slavery and has African roots. Both reggae and rap feature rival-"dissing" (disrespecting) records. The famous Jamaican series of early 1970s vinyl brawls between I Roy and Prince Jazzbo got pretty personal. "I Roy, you're a bwaoy, your teeth are like cheese," jeered Prince Jazzbo.

Among the first female rap stars, Roxanne Shante and her alter ego, the Real Roxanne, came out swinging. The Real Roxanne was conjured up to answer "Roxanne, Roxanne," by East Flatbush, Brooklyn rappers UTFO, which put down one Roxanne for being "stuck-up" and rejecting all three group members' advances. As writer Bill Adler said, "New [answering] voices were heard from and new theories advanced on a weekly basis: 'Roxanne's A Virgin,' 'Roxanne's A Man,' 'Roxanne's Little Sister,' 'Ice Roxanne,' and 'Roxanne's Doctor.' It was clear that the fever had finally burned itself out when, 'No More Roxanne, Please,' surfaced."[47]

Musicians' political philosophies and track records are as riddled with contradictions as politicians' are, and self-styled guardians of integrity often wind up exposing their own inconsistencies. Still, as Linton Kwesi Johnson put it, "The art always transcends the artist."

108

Opposite and following spread: James Brown London 1985

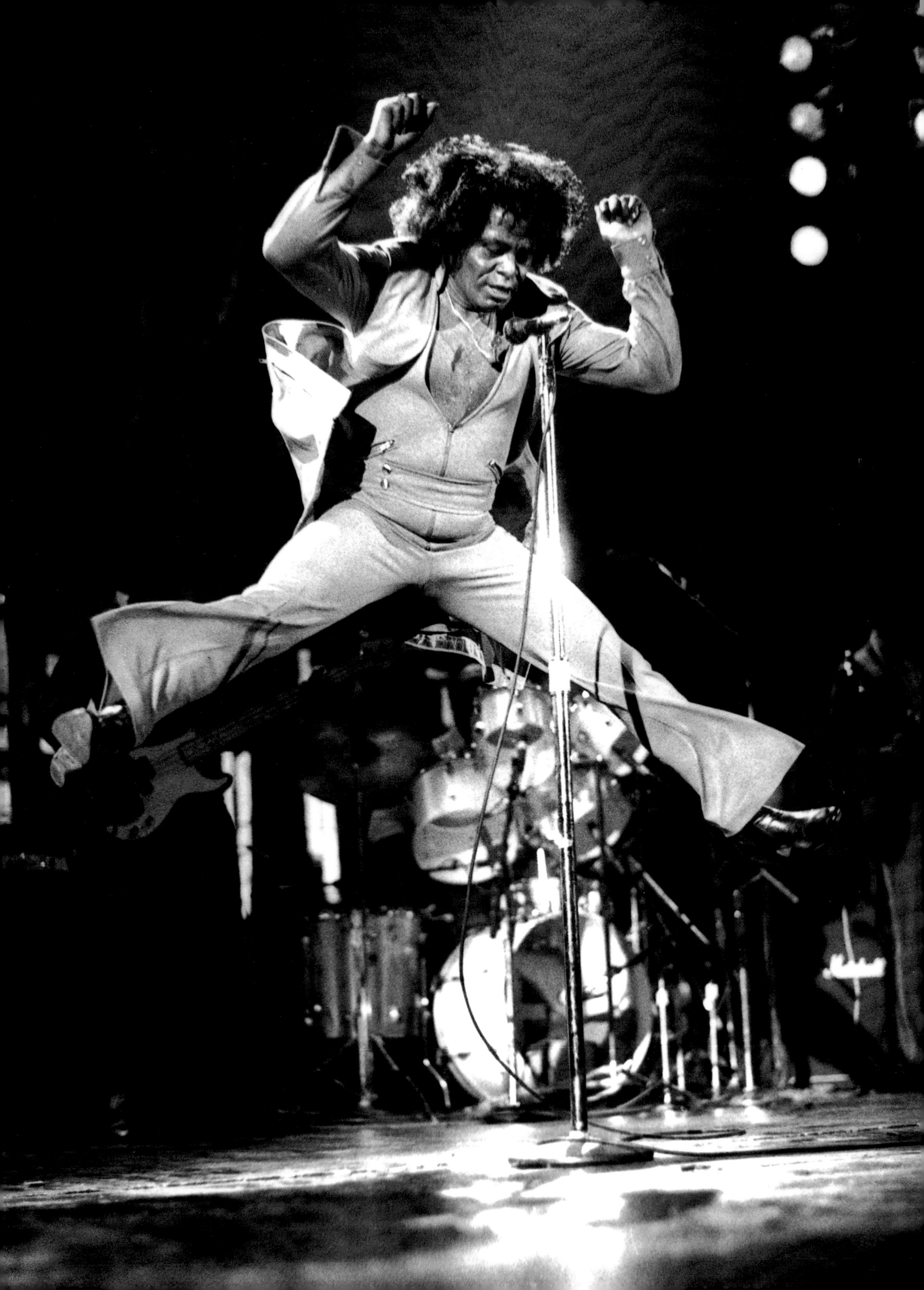

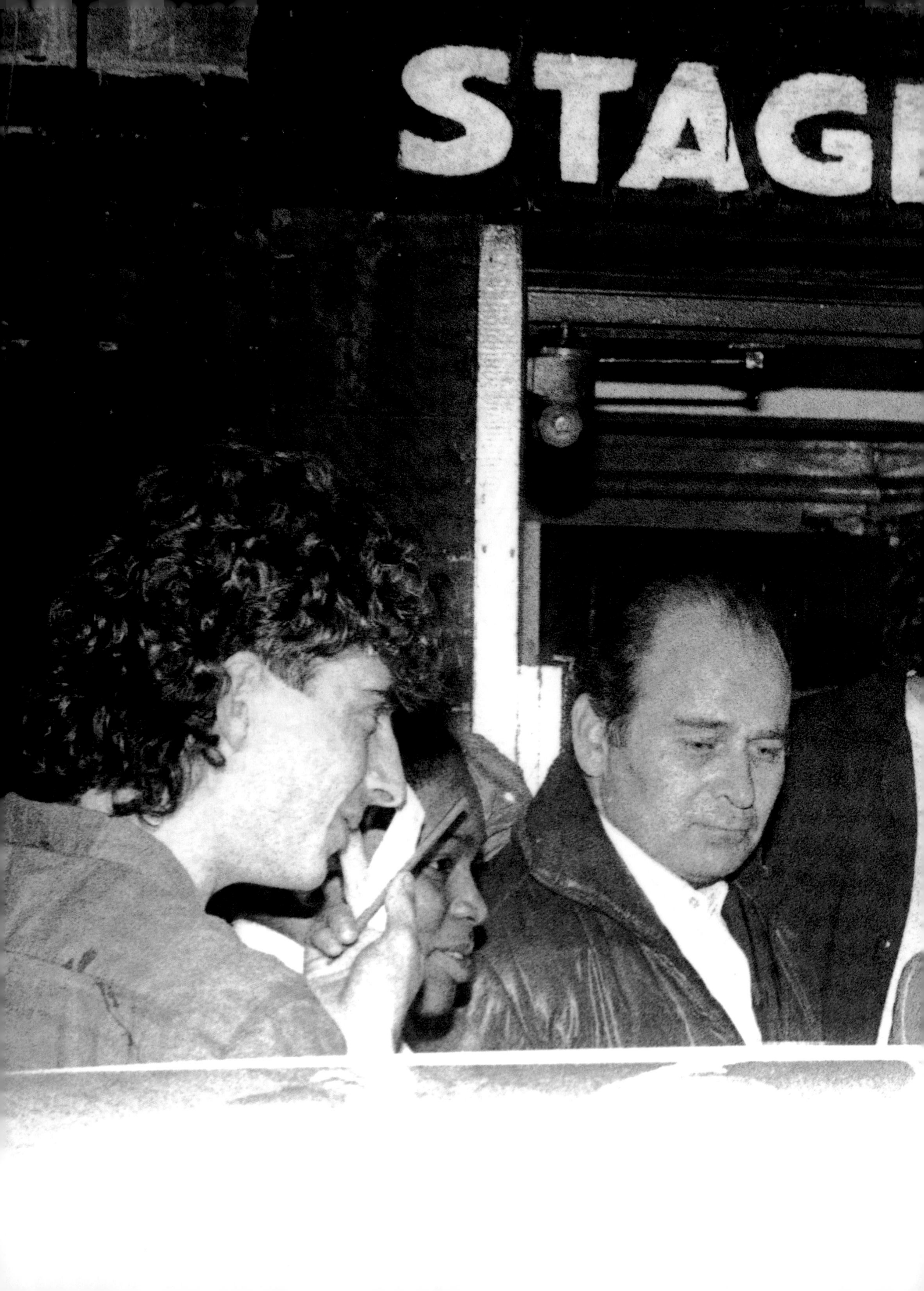
STAGE

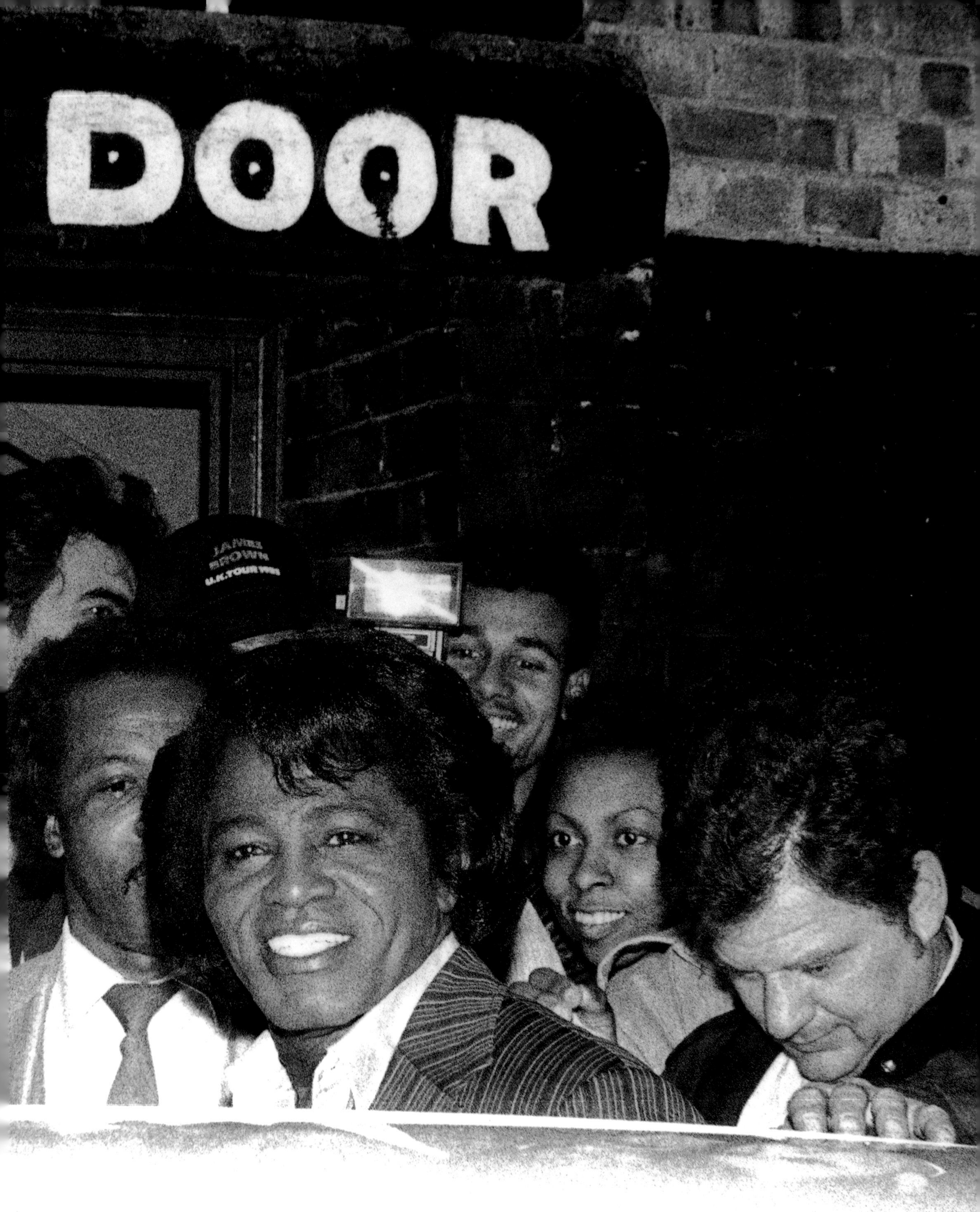
DOOR

London 1987
Bobby Byrd & Vicki Anderson

Maceo Parker London 1985

London 1986

## Temptations

Calling himself the Teacher, KRS-1 is acclaimed for having rebuilt his life from an adolescent stint in a homeless shelter to being an advocate of "Edutainment," a hybrid of education and entertainment. A cofounder of the Stop The Violence movement, he lectures at colleges and has published his own rap manual *The Science of Rap*. Yet in one famous incident, KRS-1 and his posse threw the singer of P.M. Dawn, Prince Be, off the stage at his own gig.

Though he's since redrawn his position, KRS-1 was protecting what he felt were correct rap aesthetics. P.M. Dawn had sampled the White British fashion-conscious boy band Spandau Ballet on its hit "Set Adrift On Memory Bliss." To add to this controversy, in a philosophical interview, Prince Be had tried to explain that our spiritual selves were just as important as the bodies in which they were housed, and went so far as to postulate that he wasn't Black. He meant that we are all universal beings, but for KRS-1, Prince Be was a traitor to the Black man. The irony was that each man was defending his own idea of revolution.

Although rap often suggested a hard-core, macho domain, sensitivity came through in outfits like Guru's Gang Starr and the Digable Planets with their jazz-inflected rap. For Atlanta's laid-back, daishiki-wearing Arrested Development, the new South was a bohemian Eden, where they reclaimed the country ways that had been passé since the blues had gone electric. But both the homespun Arrested Development and P.M. Dawn's utopian idealism were at odds with the prevailing trends of the macho, "Mack Daddy" badman.

"Blaxploitation was the first time we ever had a Black hero on the screen, instead of just playing a subservient role, like butlers or chauffeurs," recalled Isaac Hayes. "You had a Black guy that was a hero, so whatever he did, people loved it. After a while, some people became a bit concerned that it was giving the wrong image to the Black community" But what they didn't know was that any movie genre in its infancy is going to be exploitative. But blaxploitation didn't have time to expand. Hollywood backed off, thereby paving the way for hood survival movies and soundtracks such as Mayfield's *Superfly* and Bobby Womack's *Across 110th Street*. Isaac Hayes created *Shaft*, popularizing the guitar sound of "Wah Wah" Watson. He looked like no singer before—half wrestler, half gladiator,

114

Stevie Wonder, London 1984

with a shaved head and gold chains draped across his torso. His next incarnation was no less dramatic; robed as "Black Moses" he reminded all people of what color those folks in the Bible really were.

In the 1960s, groups like the Last Poets touched a generation. In their self-depictions as superhustlers, there was a nobility about the Last Poets that touched the young Linton Kwesi Johnson, a first-generation Briton from a Jamaican family. "I loved the way their poetry spoke to the condition of Black people in America by using street language and percussion. I had no idea poetry could be like that."

Well aware of their role as a bridge between separated members of a pan-African diaspora, the Last Poets' inflammatory rhymes used African drums with an urgency that galvanized. Their stark drama was influential even when their records were out of print and becoming prized rarities. These raging prophets were torn by their own internal conflicts, making them true representatives of a fractured society. Rival factions laid claim to the name Last Poets, originally taken from a poem by Willie Kgositsile, a South African poet. Some fell down the tunnel of crack or were arrested for guns before rising again as elder statesmen of rap.

The Los Angeles poetry and jazz movement to which the Last Poets belonged included the Watts Prophets Don Cherry, Ornette Coleman, and Jayne Cortez. In her vivid, percussive style, Jayne Cortez hefted this battering ram at Western world attitudes toward Nigeria, "They want the oil, but they don't want the people," over a pell-mell hurtle of free drums played by her son, Denardo Coleman. Though she never made music with her ex-husband Ornette Coleman, they share the same belief in owning their work and creating outlets to maintain creative freedom. As Denardo put it, "Don't wait for the call, just go ahead and create."[48]

There is no separation between Cortez's many self-published CDs and books of verse and her political activity such as organizing academic conferences and grass-roots literacy programs. She participated in voter registration in the South for SNCC and marched with baby Denardo and worked with South Africa's African National Congress. Cortez has seen progress in the issues she has raised. Referring to a 1990 track, she laughed, "We can't play [songs like] 'Mandela Is Coming,' any more, because he's already come!"

115

Last Poets London 1985

Arrested Development Atlanta 1992

Ice T **New York 1993**

Public Enemy **London 1987**

Jerry Dammers's *Free Nelson Mandela* was one of the albums that agitated the release of South Africa's hero. In the same campaign, Brian Jackson and Gil Scott-Heron recorded "Johannesburg." "When he got out, people said, 'Gil, you did "Johannesburg" too soon.' I said, 'Well, hell, the brother had been in jail for twelve years....I bet he didn't think it was too soon!"[49]

At nineteen years old, Scott-Heron published his first novel, *The Vulture*, followed by *The Nigger Factory*. His verbal panache made titles like "The Revolution Will Not Be Televised," into popular catchphrases.

Both Cortez and Scott-Heron inspired Linton Kwesi Johnson. "I came to poetry out of politics, out of my involvement with the Black Panther movement. It was different from the American party, rooted in the Caribbean anti-colonial struggle," remembered Johnson. "The poems I wrote came out of struggles, like "The Forces of Victory," which was the name of a Notting Hill Carnival mas (masquerade) we played when we'd stopped the attempted cancellation of Carnival. "Reggae Fi Peach" was about a white teacher, Blair Peach, who was killed in a fight with the National Front."

The horrible death of Jamaican poet Michael Smith in 1983 underlines the potential impact of a cultural agitator. When Johnson traveled to Jamaica in 1975 he found a community of young "dub poets" experimenting with Rasta Kumina drums and the vivacious cadence of original DJs like Big Youth and U Roy. "It made me feel that what I'd been doing all these years had some validity, that I wasn't a freak," Johnson said. The poetry scene he found in Jamaica was centered around the Jamaican School of Drama, where the key poets were the students Jean "Binta" Breeze, Oku Onuora, and Michael Smith. Johnson described Smith as "the greatest performer of poetry I've seen in my entire life.

"Within this poetry you have sound system culture," said Smith. "King Tubby's (a nightclub) was a place where DJs always rock about social problems that was happening inside the country and so the dance always served as a groundation point for reasoning (discussion)."

The outspoken Smith won an international audience with his electric first album, *Mi Cyaan Believe It*. But his concerns remained Jamaican.

Prince Jazzbo London 1988

KRS-1 London 1988

Roxanne Shante London 1989

# P.M. Dawn
New York 1993

Mutabaruka — London 1983

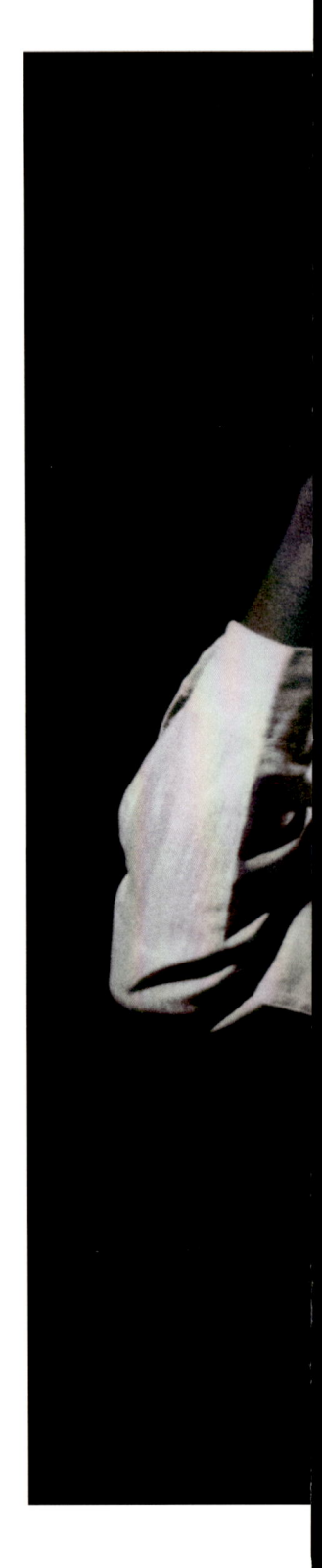

Linton Kwesi Johnson — London 1984

Gil Scott-Heron — London 1984

Oku Onura — London 1983

120

London 1981  Michael Smith

121

The day after he heckled a government official at a Jamaica Labor Party (JLP) meeting, Smith was stoned to death by JLP supporters in the Stony Hill area of Kingston.

Perhaps the most brutally ironic story among all these poetic revolutionaries is that of the lanky, charismatic people's poet, Mzwakhe Mbuli, whose trenchant growl on "Change Is Pain," proved an accurate prediction.

During the years leading up to the release of Nelson Mandela, Mzwakhe was living underground, yet still dared to recite works like "Change Is Pain" at funerals of ANC activists, one of the few places a crowd could gather. His unmistakable basso profundo introduced Mandela at his inauguration. Yet under ANC rule, Mzwakhe was jailed in maximum security for an alleged robbery attempt on a liquor store and a bank whose security camera had mysteriously broken down that day.

There are many ways to lose a leader. It was a combination of events and political violence that had first caused Bob Marley to flee from his home, an old colonial mansion in uptown Kingston, after gunmen busted in and tried to shoot him, wounding his manager, Don Taylor in 1976.

After the assassination attempt, Marley left the island for years. Taking temporary refuge in London in 1977, the Soul Rebel explained his new cheerful direction with his album *Kaya*.

"After the shooting...me never want to...to just t'ink about shooting. So me just ease up me mind and go in a different bag. What me stand for me always stand for. Jah is my strength. Ten, twelve years me a sing. Am I always gonna sing about aggression and frustration and captivity and all dem t'ing? Well now, you think it's my pride to really keep on doing that? The thing is, that must end when it must end. Me no gwan sing about dat. Me is ahead. Not a head of a people," he cautiously interrupted himself, mindful as ever of misinterpretation, "but ahead of certain things. How long must I sing the same song?"[50]

Nonetheless, Bob Marley continued to make militant music until his death from cancer in 1981 at thirty-three years old. The Wailers set the tone for reggae's militant style. Theirs was rebel music, and while American soul bands were wearing silver jumpsuits, the Wailers flashed army fatigues, ready for the revolution.

The most outspoken and abrasive Wailer was the lanky Peter Tosh. On April 22, 1978, at the Peace Concert held to celebrate a truce between the warring JLP and PNP downtown vigilantes, Tosh showed the stitches in his head where he'd been beaten by the police "beast." "Talking 'bout pirates," he harangued the audience, which included the Prime Minister Michael Manley and the opposition leader Edward Seaga, with a rant against government hypocrisy and police brutality. It was an appropriate introduction to his "Equal Rights and Justice," and Tosh defiantly smoked a gigantic "spliff" onstage, singing, "Legalize it and I will advertise it." Tosh was killed along with his friend the DJ Free-I in his St. Catherine home by a disgruntled acquaintance.

In as volatile an island as Jamaica, artists are forced to tread a delicate path to avoid being co-opted by the two rival parties or risk the consequences. This feat was accomplished by the former child star Dennis Brown, whose song "Revolution" managed to be melodic, militant—and nonpartisan. When a number of PNP supporters were rounded up and shot on a beach by the army, the extrovert Big Youth, known for his shattering yowl on "Screaming Target," publicized it with his "Green Bay Massacre." One of the finest island voices, Inner Circle's Jacob Miller rampaged around the stage in army fatigues as he pelted social commentary like "Tired Fe Lick Weed In A Bush" and "Tenement Yard."

Many groups of the time wore "Jah Chic": khakis and the Rasta colors red, green, and gold. But stepping high in the dance style of the day, Puma, a Rasta woman from Harlem, gave a visual charge to the harmony trio Black Uhuru that set them apart. Their sound was uncompromising, with revolutionary-style songs such as "Plastic Smile" and "General Pententiary." The voice of Michael Rose strutted and prowled and was highlighted by Puma's and Duckie Simpson's vocals. It was all anchored in the powerhouse grooves and dubs of Jamaica's dominant rhythm section, drummer Sly Dunbar and bass player, Robbie Shakespeare. It seemed that Black Uhuru would be the "militant" band to spread the message in Marley's footsteps, but as soon as they won a Grammy in 1984, the trio split, torn by internal arguments.

As Puma discovered when she left Harlem for Jamaica, the struggle for Tosh's "Equal Rights and Justice" happens everywhere. In England, the reggae band Aswad also found that wearing army uniforms expressed their feeling of being in the firing line every day. Relations between Black youth and the police were volatile, and a Napoleonic anti-vagrancy law known as Sus, was a frequent excuse to give innocent young Black males a police record. Inevitably, the members of Aswad themselves experienced run-ins with Sus, and their first single "Three Babylon Try and Make I and I Run," was part of a climate of protest that eventually led to the revocation of the law.

As Bob Marley sang in his track "Punky Reggae Party," there was considerable community activity between punk rockers and second generation reggae acts such as London's Southall community activists Misty In Roots and Birmingham's Steel Pulse. The first black band to play the "in" punk club the Vortex, Steel Pulse was unusual in its theatricality. The members donned Ku Klux Klan robes for their song of the same name. Fascist activity was at a height, and the synergy between punks and dreads encouraged the foundation of the effective antiracist organization Rock Against Racism.

A revolution can involve beliefs as well as politics. "There is a hankering for the spiritual again in Jamaica after the materialism of the '80s," reported Linton Kwesi Johnson in 1998. The socially conscious reggae tradition begun by Marley and extended by Aswad was picked up again by artists like Luciano, who, like Salif Keita in Mali, was once homeless. Given to periods of solitary meditation, Luciano's voice is rich on songs like "It's Me Again, Jah." Sharing Luciano's producer—Xterminator, aka Philip "Fattis" Burrell—Anthony B blends singing and toasting, wearing the towering headwrap of the "Bobo Dreads" group of Rastas.

In contrast to traditional African praise songs, where everything is always, of necessity, wonderful, many other African artists are political commentators.

To draw attention to the mass deportations of West African immigrants, both Salif Keita and Youssou N'Dour wrote rousing anthems that effectively mobilized people to action. N'Dour's *"Immigres"* and Keita's *"Nou Pas Bouger"* (We shall not move) gave focus to the anti-racist movement, SOS Racisme, headed by Harlem Desir.

Keita and N'Dour were thinking globally. "I played Cuban music because the people at the time liked to dance to it. I needed to go through this music to go toward the music I believed in, *mbalax*,"[51] said N'Dour.

But on a local level, after colonialism, developing countries were set on finding a music to express their new identity, usually incorporating ancestral folk rhythms.

The Wailers's roots-rock reggae sparked a musical reappraisal across the Caribbean. Comparatively prosperous French territories, the islands of Guadeloupe and Martinique, suffered from the lack of a native cultural personality, which differed from Jamaica's grinding social chasms. "When I heard the Wailers," reminisced bass player Jacob Desvarieux, who cofounded the influential group Kassav, "I thought to myself, 'why can't we take our own island rhythms, like the *gwo ka* (a stuttering drum rhythm) and make it modern.'" The result was an exhilarating groove called *zouk*, ablaze with horns and a tropical storm of bass and percussion that influenced music across the Caribbean and South America. Even Miles Davis dug *zouk*, particularly the Kassav big band that bred artists like singer Jocelyne Beroard.

Boukman Eksperyans, a voodoo rock band, also looked to ancestral inspiration. They took the name of the rebel voodoo priest who started a slave revolt in Haiti that led to the island's independence from France in 1804. In his spirit, they took the "rara" rhythms of Carnival and turned them into a music of revolution against the old Duvalier dictatorship. Their Creole patois song, *"Kalfou Danjere,"* (Dangerous Crossroads) was not banned for its reference to the voodoo and Yoruba belief that the material and spirit worlds collide at the crossroads, but for its thinly disguised critique of the government. "We're talking about the revolution. Boukman represents a cultural movement. Some Haitians in the military...are involved with the African religion voodoo, so they know the power of those cultural things,"[52] commented band member Lolo.

When the Fugees played a fund-raising show in Haiti, they insisted on having Boukman Eksperyans on the bill, despite government objections. When Jamaica became independent in 1962, the fizz of ska captured that exultant moment of nationhood, when new possibilities beckoned. The ska sound was created by Coxsone Dodd and guitarist Ernest Ranglin. Dodd chuckles as he recalls how he was in the studio with his house band and the tape machine started to speed up. The musicians dug the unexpected rhythm and began to riff off it. The result, a quirky one-drop, had shades of New Orleans barrel-house boogie-woogie, and the steaming Southern R&B that would come pumping, distorted, from transistor radios in tenement yards and wooden "rediffusion" radio boxes mounted on the walls of rum shacks. Dodd's studio band became known as

Big Youth
London 1987

London 1991

# u Roy

125

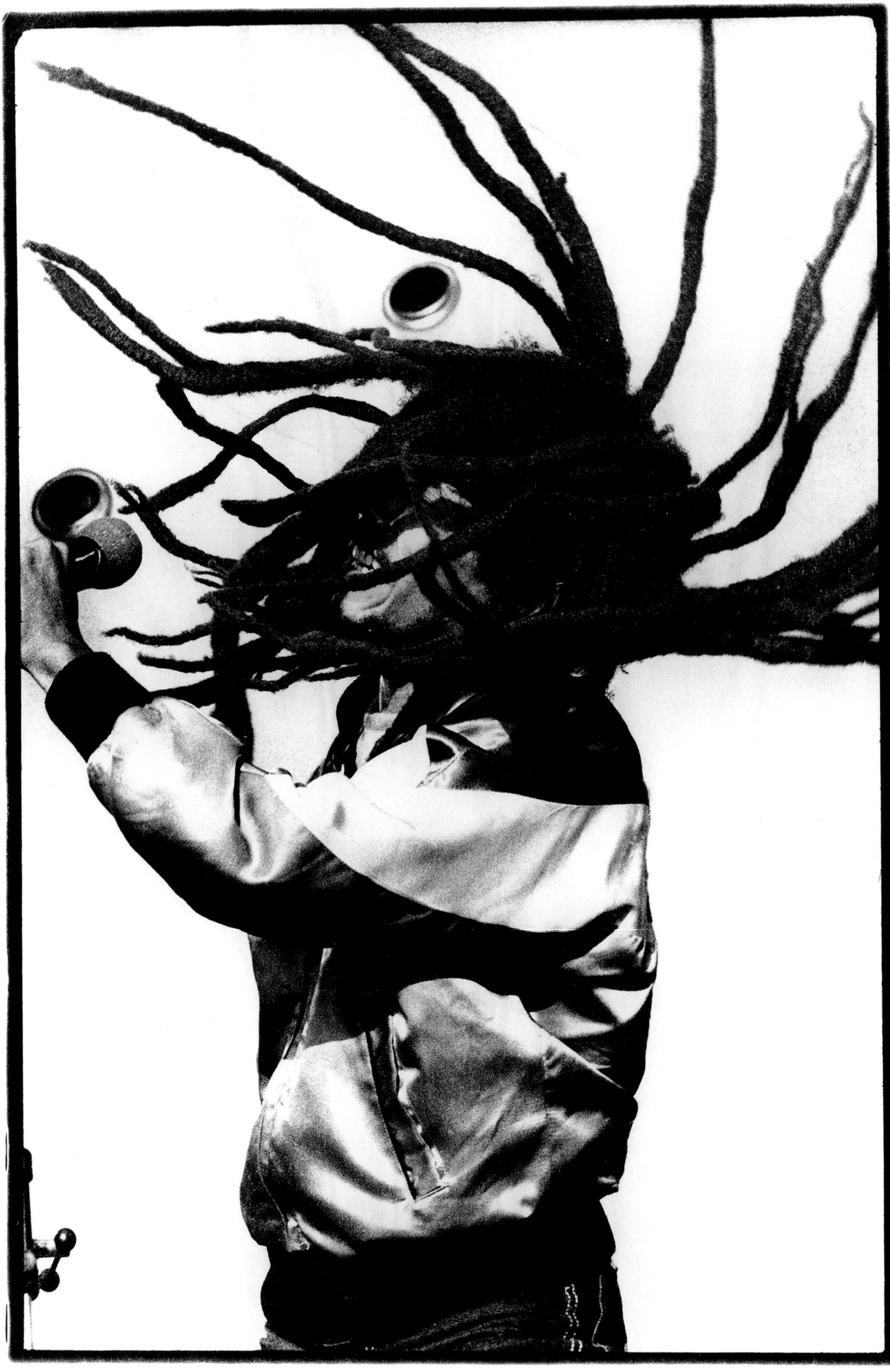

the Skatalites and the music became ska, after the choppy offbeat of the rhythm guitar.

The tragic fate of their visionary trombonist Don Drummond cut short the Skatalites' first incarnation. The shy musician with the melancholy sound was schizophrenic. Unhinged, he killed his lover, the Lebanese rhumba dancer, Margarita Mahfood.

The Skatalites disbanded shortly after this tragedy but later reformed as the popularity of their jaunty ska beat continued to grow in Britain. Multiracial, two-tone bands such as Selecter and the Beat emerged in the 1970s; and in the 1990s, the "Third Wave" of ska developed in the United States with bands like No Doubt. From a national music, ska became a global code for cheeky rude boys and girls.

Across the African continent, music played different roles in the continuing turmoil of post-colonial development. Fighting the guerilla war against Ian Smith's Rhodesian regime in the 1960s, the teenage fighters who were charged up on dagga (marijuana) and imminent gunfire listened to Bob Marley and Thomas Mapfumo's Chimurenga music on their portable music players—they were soundtracks to the revolution. "It was a pain in my heart that I was doing copycat music—covers of English and American songs."[53] Mapfumo recalled. He devised a hypnotic national liberation sound, Chimurenga, using his rock experience and traditional *m'bira* thumb-piano plus his knack for a strong melodic hook. Mapfumo was banned and jailed, but survived.

Around his neck, Nigerian Fela Anikulapo-Kuti wore a soft pouch which he would point to and say, "I have death in my pouch. They can't kill me."[54] But they did try. Fela was the outspoken critic of corruption—from colonialism, multinationals, and three Nigerian presidents, Obasanjo, Babangida and Abacha. He rolled right over them with his searing, relentlessly churning Afrobeat. Songs like "Zombie," "I.T.T." (International t'ief t'ief), and "Upside Down" defused the military mindset.

Living in Los Angeles in the 1960s with a Black Panther woman politicized Fela. During their relationship he devised a sound called Afrobeat by mixing powerful Nigerian drums with James Brown-style horns and his own "free" blasts of saxophone and a Rhodes keyboard. In 1977, Fela's seventy-eight year old mother Funmilayo, a feminist who agitated for the vote and visited Mao in China, died after she was thrown out of a window during a government raid on Fela's compound, the Kalakuta Republic. This was not the only atrocity that occurred under General Obasanjo's junta. The Kalakuta Republic was burned,

London 1980

the women savagely raped, and Fela's music and equipment destroyed. After this tragedy, Fela married twenty-seven wives in a single traditional ceremony. Many of them, faces painted and hips grinding, sang and danced on his packed stage. Finally, Fela withdrew into the spiritual African studies that had long intrigued him. Yet again, he was arrested and beaten, this time on a marijuana charge, in 1997. The military government tried to humiliate him by parading him in handcuffs on TV, but he was released after a public outcry. Four months later, he died due to years of torture and abuse as well as the HIV virus. His son Femi continues Fela's work.

Some years before, Fela had prophesied, "With the self-insight I got in the States, I vowed I was going into politics. I also saw the power I could have through music. . . . I said I would die in the struggle."[55]

127

Following page: Peter Tosh London 1981

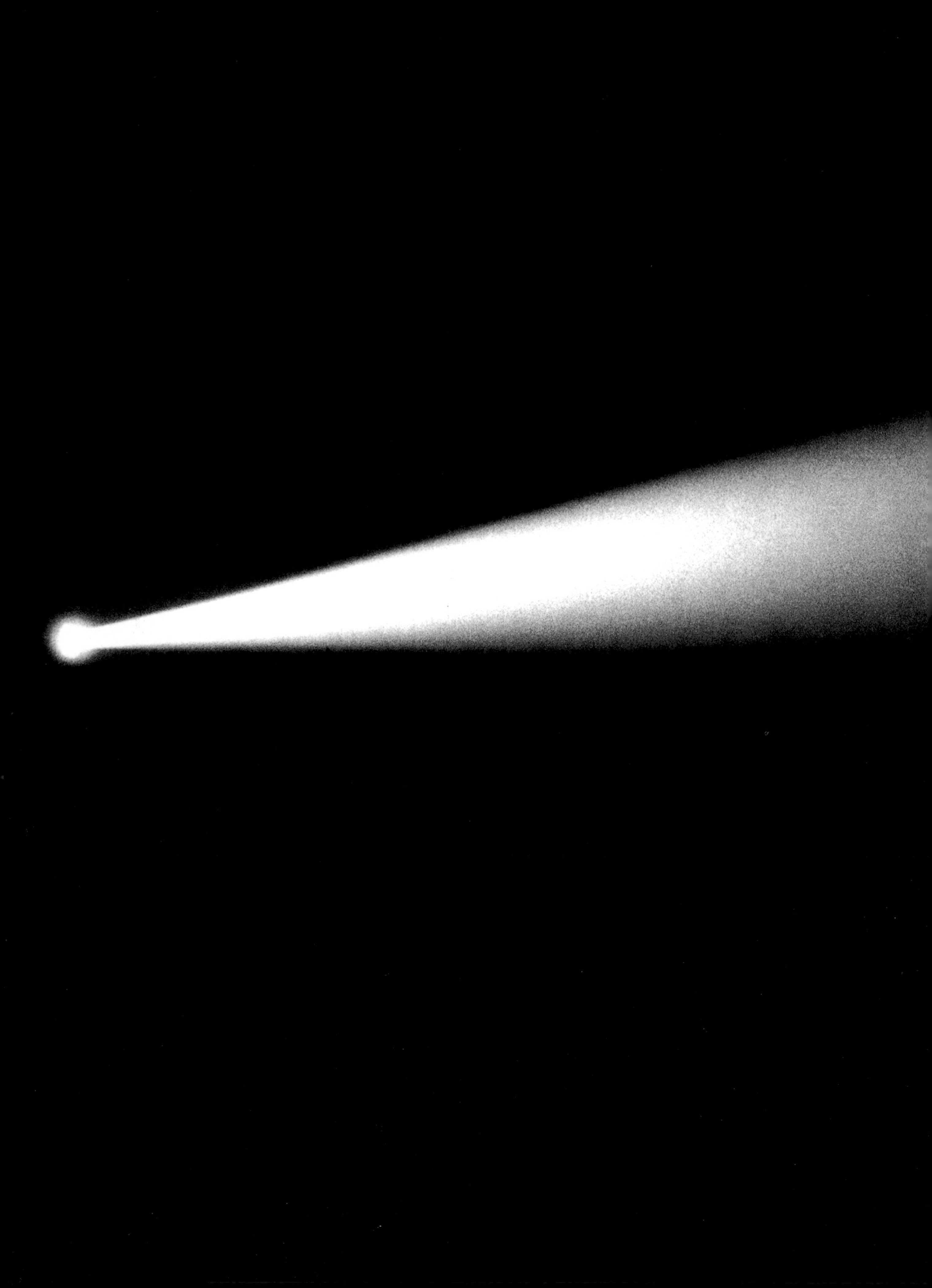

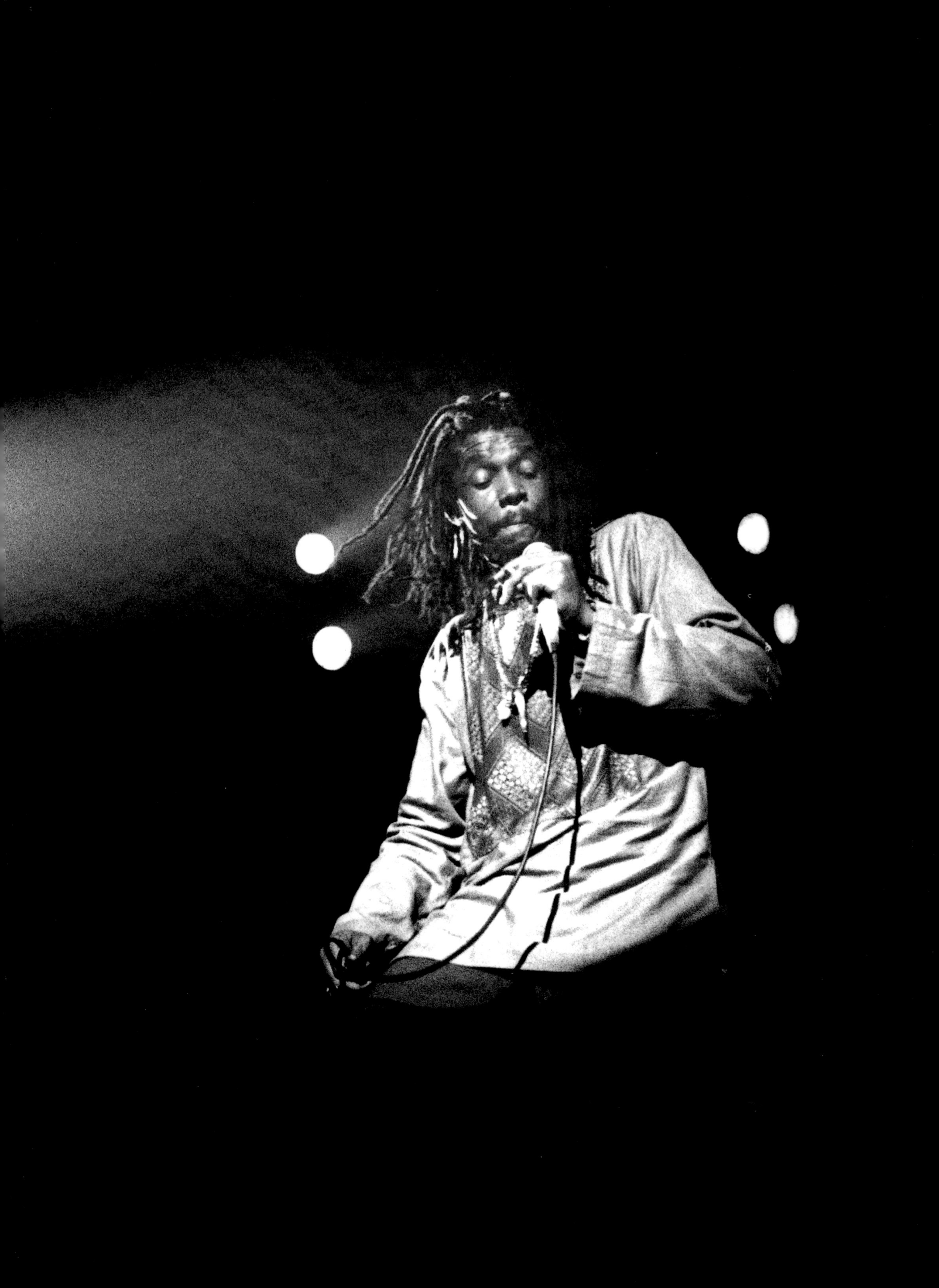

London 1980  Jacob Miller

Steel Pulse
London 1984

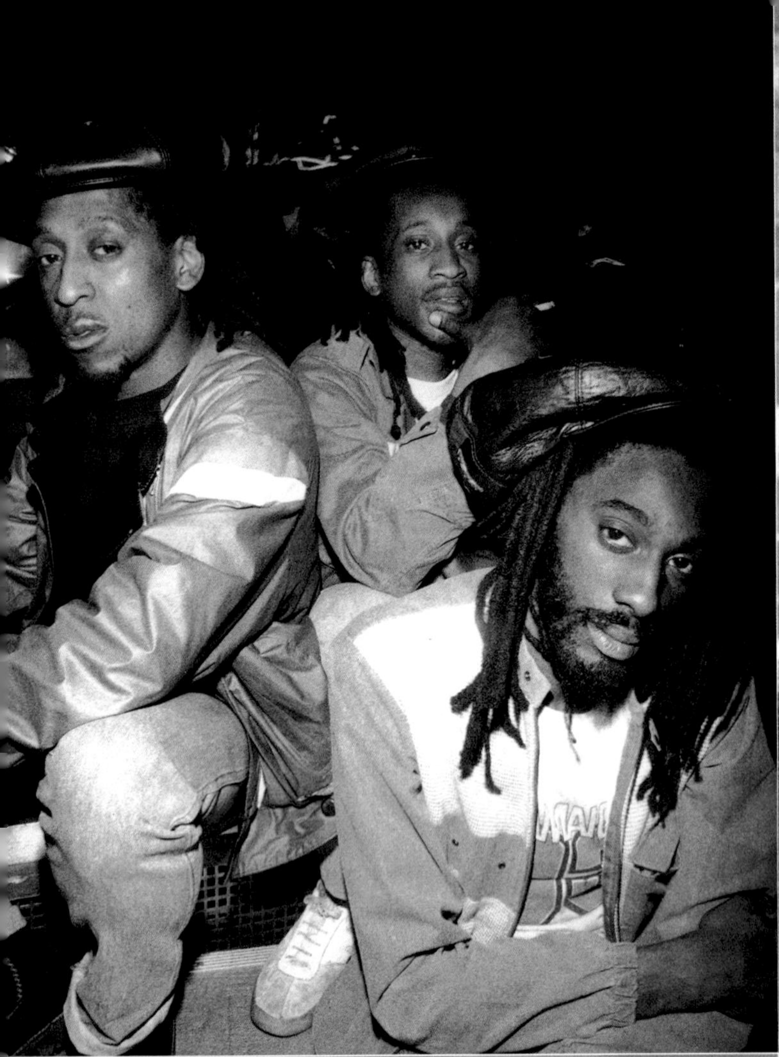
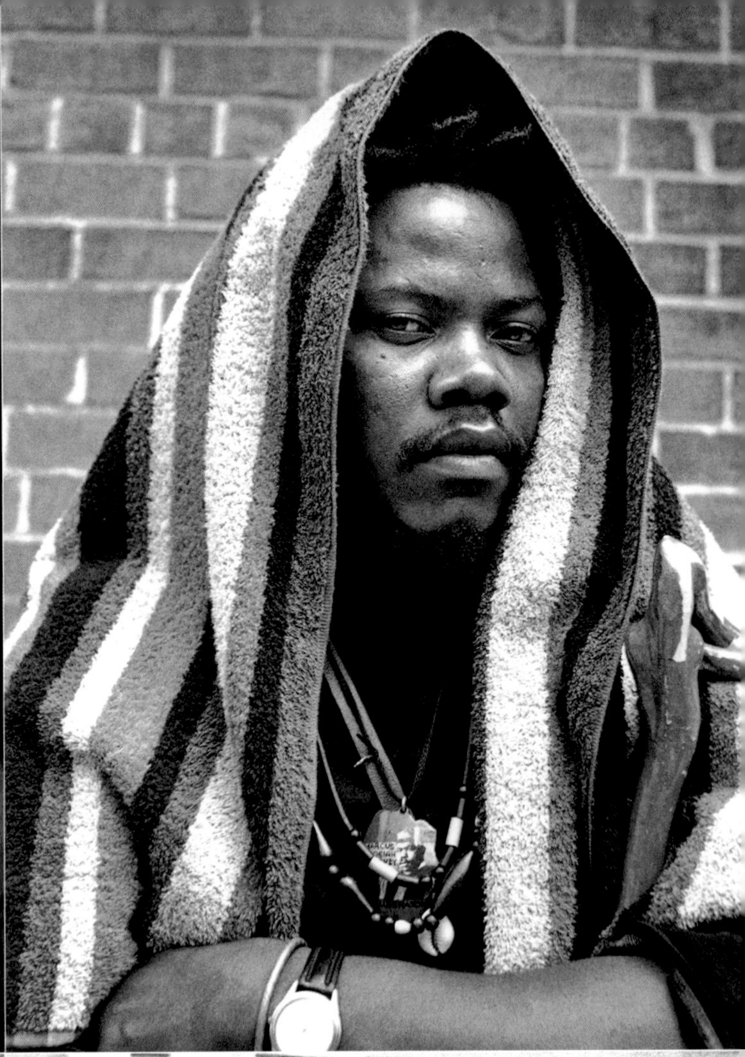
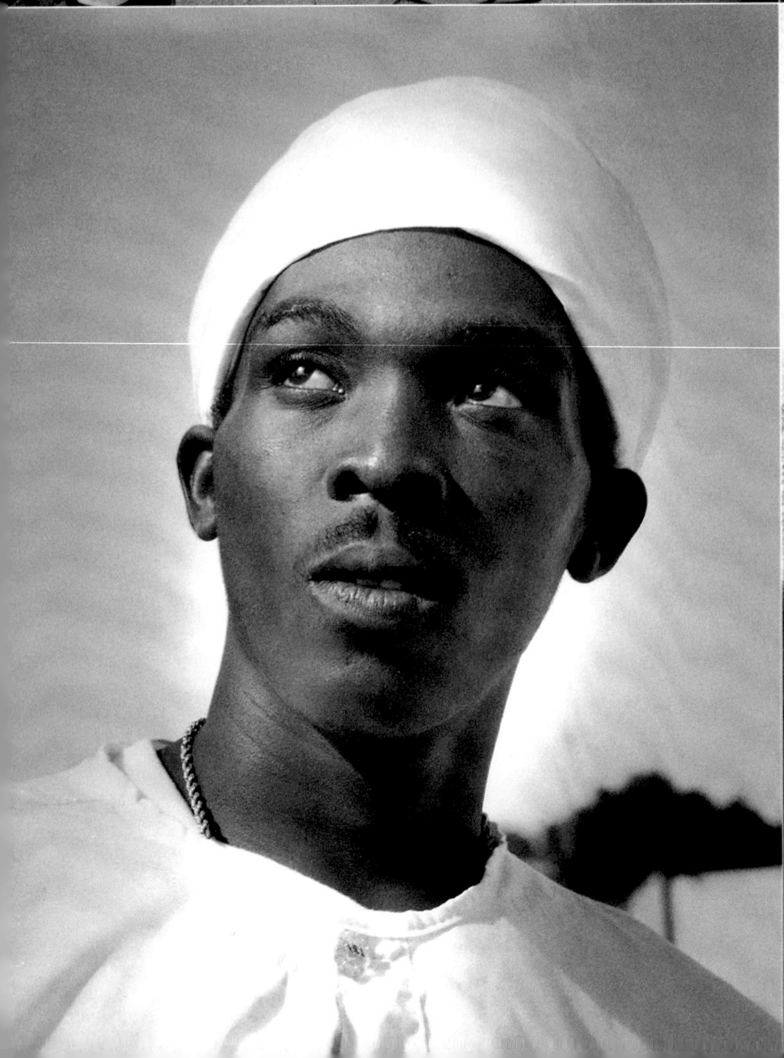
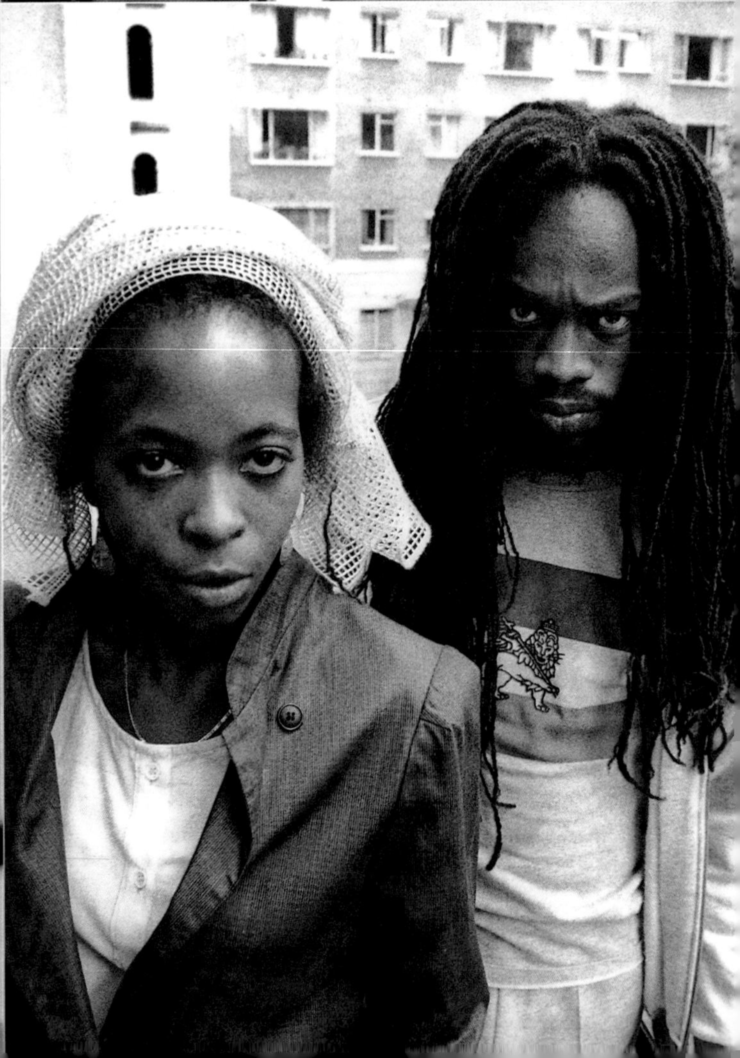

Clockwise from upper left: Aswad, Raintree, England 1984   Luciano, New York 1995   Black Uhuru, London 1983   Anthony B, New York 1997   Following page: Boukman Ekspeyrans, London 1993

Skatalites, New York 1993

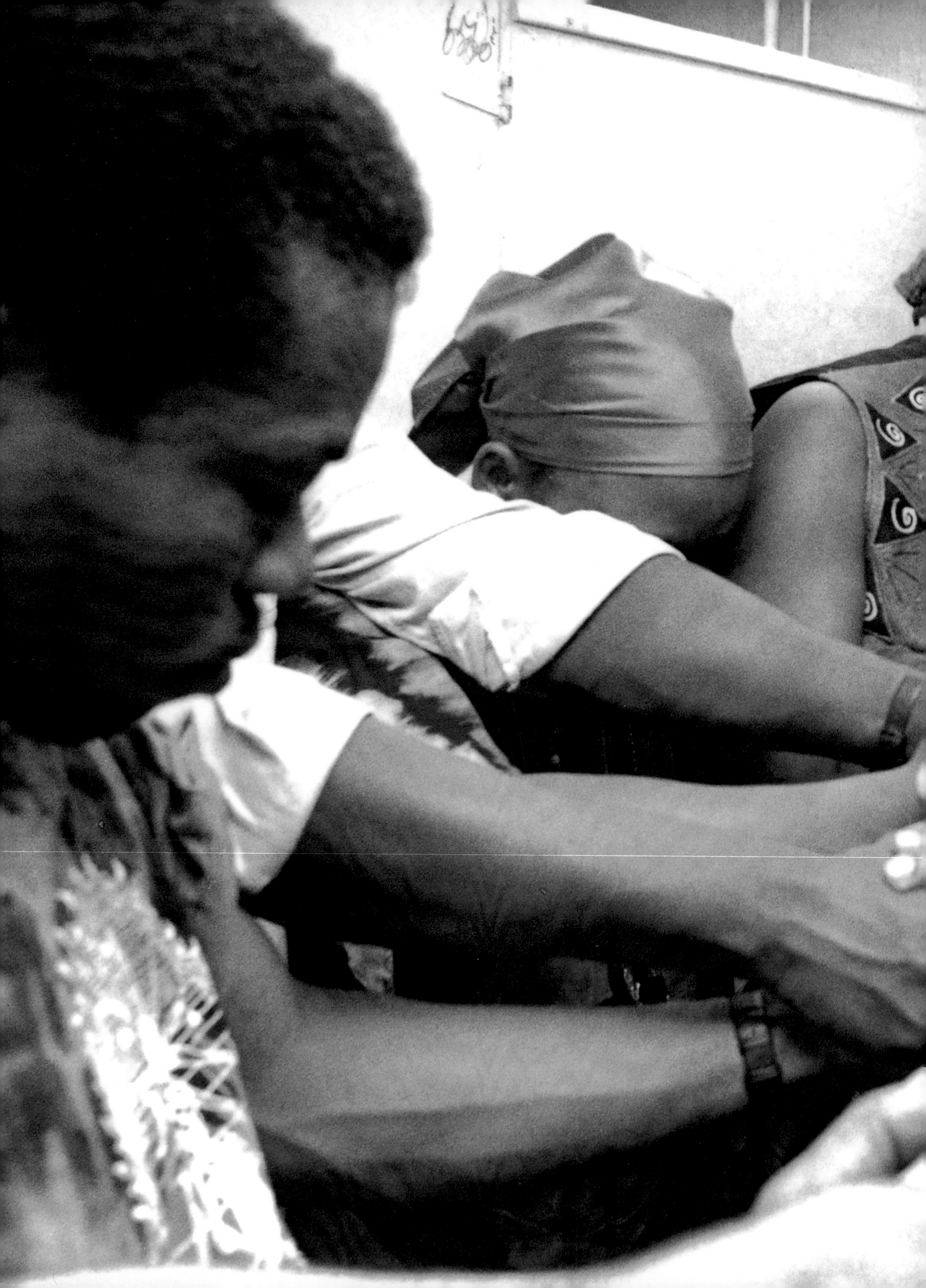

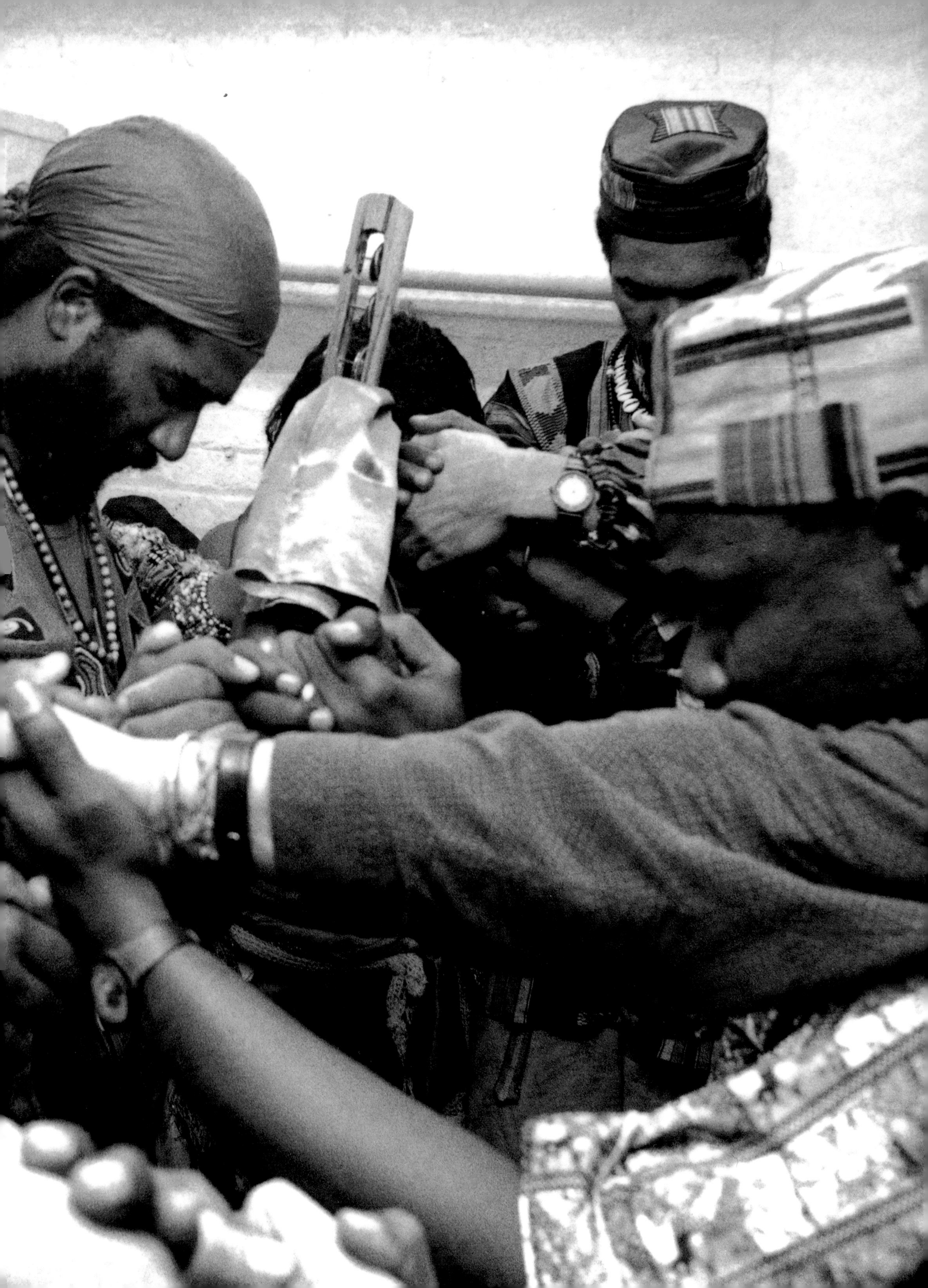

explore

Foday Musa Susa   London 1984

EXPLORERS

The black chord exists in a state of perpetual self-renewal. The process of evolution can be kick-started by just one individual who finds a special way to tell their own truth and can make others tune in. The saxophonist Ornette Coleman found his truth in a sound that meant equality, a getaway from Western musical conventions. With musicians such as trumpet player Don Cherry, Coleman broke free from four-four bars and created his "harmolodic" free jazz style.

Coleman is clear about the process of developing a musical language, "I am exchanging rhythm for notes and notes for rhythm and give them equal position. Sometimes it's challenging to do it, because the rhythms don't have to be resolved. The notes seem to always want to be spelled out."[56]

Sensing a need for the same move at the same time, a group of musicians may find their next progression together. In the 1970s, Earth, Wind, and Fire created a new style; in the 1980s, the Black Rock Coalition, a collective of artists, rocked out heavy-metal like Led Zeppelin.

Often motivated by exclusivity, keeping a defiant beat ahead of society's pack, music can become the language of an era's "state of mind." The case of 1950s Cuban/American, beatnik-hipster Slim Gaillard's own "vout-eroonie" language showed that being on the edge can be vout-talottafun.

"Why do we hear the things we hear?" reflected guitarist/producer and cofounder of the Black Coalition Vernon Reid of the group Living Colour. "Part of creativity is to find a new context in which to put the experiences we call emotion and to express inexpressible things. How they're expressed is a function of the context of what's really going on—conflicts, forces in opposition, the amount of resources that are available at a particular time to particular people."

Both African American rap and Jamaican reggae and its spacey sister dub began by expressing their local experience but echoed globally. Building on Jamaican sound system culture, hip-hop began as an underground minority music, by and for a materially disadvantaged crowd in the Bronx. Its rise coincided with funding cuts in the school system's music budgets. Kids who no longer had access to studying a musical instrument began playing record decks instead of keyboards. An economical music for an impoverished island, dub enables one track to be recycled over and over again.

King Tubby stumbled upon the idea of dub. It was furthered by others such as Niney the Observer, Augustus Pablo with his wistful Far Eastern style, and the wiry, diminutive Lee "Scratch" Perry, who got his start on Coxsone Dodd's sound system.

A myth grew up around Scratch in direct relation to both his sound—it gave a riveting originality to many artists including Max Romeo, the Heptones, the Congoes and Junior Murvin—and the rumors of his increasingly eccentric behavior. In Jamaica, DJ's were called "toasters," and Scratch planted a row of toasters along his fence like so many traitors' heads.

"Dreadlocks is dreadful and dread times is too dread,"[57] he declared in 1979 when, disillusioned with Rasta, he changed his name to Pipecock Jackson. In this volatile new persona he painted every wall of his Black Ark Studio with fractured words and enormous X's, a symbol that he said was the creative power of the universe.

There was undeniable genius in the flashing of his fingers as he deftly twisted a dub out of the four faders on his basic recording machine. Taking all the tracks on which a song's instruments and voices were recorded, he would raise or lower their volume, varying the speed, twisting echo and reverb dials to make individual sounds fly in, flare up, and be gone. From within one song, Perry would excavate another, then another, giving different dimensions to its landscape each time.

Surprise is as key an ingredient in a dub version as the bass line is in the original tune. By uncovering the nuances between reggae notes, Scratch's dubs propelled music into another dimension, redefined the limits of rhythm and dance, and refracted them into a host of new genres—house, garage, techno, rave, and hip-hop. Linton Kwesi Johnson titled an album after it: *Bass Culture*.

The seduction of the deceptively simple reggae bass as transmitted by the instrument's masters like Aston "Family Man" Barrett of the Wailers and his protégé, Robbie Shakespeare, lies in a combination of melody and suggestion, the absent notes sometimes being as loud as those played. But just as the hip bone is connected to the thigh bone, it takes two to make a rhythm section.

Sly Dunbar replaced Family Man's brother, Carlton, as Shakespeare's drummer after Carlton's murder. Sly's style goes with Robbie's just as ackee goes with saltfish, in the Jamaican national dish. They became known as the "Riddim Twins." Shakespeare elaborated, "You can play well with somebody you don't get on with, but me and Sly...I can tell you when he's going to roll and I guess he can do the same with me. We talk musically."[58]

As a team, Sly and Robbie have been rolling out hits on a conveyor belt since the 1970s. Like many Jamaican musicians of the time, their first instruments were homemade. Barrels become drums, tin cans and fishing line make a bass or guitar. As adults, both Sly and Robbie are always keen to try out the latest technology. When the first drum machines came out in the late 1970s, Sly immediately began to experiment. He added the bubbler, steppers, and the heartbeat to his list of original rhythms. Each prompted a new dance craze. Their sound was sought as an elixir by stars in search of direction, from French icon Serge Gainsbourg to the former Jamaican schoolgirl, champion track athlete Grace Jones. Together they developed the unique, androgynous Grace Jones persona, creating the pulsating "Pull Up To The Bumper" and "My Jamaican Guy." There was even an abortive session with James Brown. With the advance of techno in the late 1990s, Sly and Robbie sensibly declared themselves to be the original drum'n'bass and began experimenting with ambient and electronic textures.

The measure of a successful sound system lies not only in its selection of music, but also in its power to transmit bass so earthshattering that it practically rearranges the listeners' molecular structure. Submission to the bass was a bonding process that techno inherited from reggae. Reggae and dub have long served as a communion between Black and White culture in Britain, whose bands—like the racially mixed UB40 and the first generation Asian Brits of Asian Dub Foundation—claim reggae as their own. It's what they were raised on.

Sound systems perform an essential function, attracting followers as football teams do. Foremost among these missionaries of bass culture are sounds like Jah Jerry's Stone Love in Jamaica, or Jah Shaka in Britain.

Away from the sound-system culture, where Shaka ruled, much of Britain's reggae life was conducted in the shebeens. The name comes from Jamaica via Irish indentured laborers. Illegal all-night house parties held in derelict buildings, shebeens became a focus in the 1970s for every kind of artist and band from Culture Club to the British reggae scene's Cimarons and Matumbi, as well as Ladbroke Grove's young lions, Aswad. Without shebeens, their sound systems, and bass culture, there would have been no warehouse parties and no rave, techno, or drum'n'bass.

The pretty town of Bristol was a main slave port and has had a more consistent Black presence than most of Britain. In the blazing summer of 1981, the working-class area of St. Pauls was the scene of famous antipolice riots. A university town with nearby fields of psychedelic mushrooms, Bristol developed its own spacey, leisurely, dub-derived sound. A sense of mystery pervades Bristol's music, whether trip hop or techno. The dense textures and otherworldly ambiance of Massive Attack began as the wild bunch, a reggae sound system. At Bristol's Dug-out club, future Massive members, Tricky, 3-D, Mushroom, and Daddy

Grace Jones
New York 1998

London 1981

G. along with producer Nellee Hooper, set the tone. Shaped by dub and New York's graffiti hip-hop scene, the members of Massive Attack abhor showbiz schmoozing and turn their backs to the audience as Miles Davis did.

The slippery, whispery flow of Tricky broadcasting from the dark side was key to early Massive Attack's elusive identity. An aptly named renegade loner with a fascination for the secrets of the underworld, Tricky was obsessed with getting at the guts of his real feelings and had too much to say to stay in a band and compromise with fellow musicians.

On his own, Tricky began making brooding, ominous soundtracks to a paranoid zeitgeist that he dubbed "Pre-Millennial Tension," and satirized his own success in the record *Nearly God*.

After the departure of Tricky and their first vocalist, Shara Nelson, the Massives worked with various singers including Tracy Thorn of the group Everything But The Girl as well as Nicolette. Their constant voice, however, became Jamaican Horace Andy, a reggae veteran of Coxsone Dodd's golden era at 1960s Studio One, whose brittle falsetto adorned one of reggae's favorite tracks, "Skylarking"; a warning to all young ne'er-do-well's that, "If you keep on doing, what you all are doing, you will end up, up, up in jail."

Jamaica has a singular relationship with rap. A number of leading talents have Caribbean parents, including Busta Rhymes, Doug E. Fresh, and Eric B, of Eric B. and Rakim. Several rappers, including KRS-1, paid homage to the link by working with Jamaican toasters such as Shinehead and Shabba Ranks.

The crucible of 1970s rap was the Bronx's Rock Steady Park—as it's now known—ruled by DJ's like Kool Herc, a laconic Jamaican brother with a valuable knowledge of Kingston Sound System runnings.

Scene makers Afrika Bambaataa, Run-DMC, and Grandmaster Flash tapped electricity straight from Con Ed's overhead wires to spin the wheels of steel. They started scratching, working the same record with the label scratched off, back and forth on two decks with their fingertips, palm, or even elbow to catch a particular phrase or break of the song, and playing it over and over, making the pleasure last. It was a shot at fame and a name. Local youths would practice all week for a chance to be passed the mike for syncopated rapping over tracks, developing their own style just as Jamaican DJs like U-Roy, with his spirited whoop and the boisterous Big Youth, had in the 1960s.

The Jamaica/hip-hop connection grew. "I remember a sense of pride," said Neneh Cherry of the mid-1980s, when she pioneered the fusion of singing with rap on her single, "Buffalo Stance." "A lot of people were wearing red, gold, and green (the Rastafarian colors). Musicians were communicating between reggae and dancehall and hip-hop. People from America tried to "chat" (rap Jamaican style) in a hip-hop way. Some of it was sort of embarassing, but it was an important com-

142

Slim Gaillard
London 1984

143

munication between two cultures."

With most media, from newspapers to movies, divorced from street people and life, rap enabled around-the-way guys, regular neighborhood characters, to put across their personalities to an unprecedented extent. Early voices included Spoonie Gee, who was the nephew of R&B veterans; Bobby and Sylvia Robinson of the premier early rap labels, Enjoy and Sugar Hill. As a kid, Spoonie used to write rhymes in their apartment, and his in-house spontaneity and tongue-twisting skills encouraged the concept of the label house band the Sugar Hill Gang. "What Spoonie Gee was doing was tribal hip-hop, really raw, just beats. It blew my mind," remembered Neneh Cherry.

Another Harlem-ite, the exuberant Biz Markie, tickled with broad, grade-school humor on tracks like "Pickin' Boogers." Litigation by British singer, Gilbert O'Sullivan, whose "Alone Again, Naturally," had been sampled by Markie, slowed down the rapper's career. After a lapse in recording, Markie was championed as an old-school icon by punky hip-hoppers, the Beastie Boys.

The slow, deliberate flow of Rakim exuded wry intelligence. He and his disc-spinning partner Eric B showed an alternative to the brash, self-promotion of most early rappers. Rakim alluded laconically to an early career as a stick-up kid (mugger) while still projecting seriousness and religious awareness. As he said, "I Ain't No Joke." The stoic, expressionless Eric B innovated sampling the funk of James Brown, a soon to be common selection.

A more playful school of Afrocentric rap arose with the Native Tongues Possee in the 1980s, from artists like Queen Latifah, British rapper Monie Love, and De La Soul. "They were called 'the hippies of hip-hop' because their lyrics were not just about their block, corner, or bodega (store) it was about what was in their heads," said Neneh Cherry.

The neighborhoods described by rappers tended to be hardcore urban environments, but Jazzy Jeff and the Fresh Prince presented a cheerier landscape familiar to all middle-class youth, with endearingly naive titles like "Parents Just Don't Understand" and "Girls Ain't Nothing But Trouble." If rap records were TV series, Jazzy Jeff and the Fresh Prince would be the "Cosby Show". It is not surprising that the Fresh Prince, aka Will Smith, began his ascent into the highest ranks of screen actors with the feel-good TV series "The Fresh Prince of Bel Air," based on his lovable persona.

A history of rap could be written based on the government housing developments that artists come from. These places breed their own cultures. To glamorize their Staten Island housing development, the rappers Wu Tang Clan created their own warrior-monk mythology and dubbed their housing developments Shao-Lin. The philosophy of their parallel cosmos, in which the Wu-Tang sword prevails over all rivals, was initially gleaned from kung fu flicks, Japanese "anime" cartoons, and video and computer games. The Wu Tang Clan, including the RZA, Method Man, Raekwon, and Old Dirty Bastard, aka Big Baby Jesus, are a model of social organization in which members also pursue outside projects. Among these projects is the RZA's "horrorcore" group the Gravediggaz, formed with rappers Poetic, Fruikwan, and producer Prince Paul. "The life we live is like a horror movie,"[59] explained the Rza, flaunting the gold, fake fangs that are part of his Gravediggaz persona.

When the the Fugees' Wyclef Jean landed in America from Haiti, he said, "I had a picture that the minute I got to the airport, there was gonna be dollar bills flying from the sky. Instead I ended up in a place called Marlborough Projects, on Coney Island."[60] Despite his initial disillusionment, Wyclef grew up to possess plenty of dollar bills with the Fugees. Unlike most rap outfits, whose musical backing comes from DJs and sampled sounds from other records, the Fugees incorporated live instruments into their music and presented a view of the streets steeped in a sense of morality. After working together for many years, the old friends' rich sense of heritage and authenticity flowered in their breakthrough track, a sparse interpretation of Roberta Flack's evergreen "Killing Me Softly," whose main adornment was Hill's lush delivery.

The prototype for rappers working together as a family unit was laid out by Afrika Bambaataa, who boosted his Bronx River pride in the early days of rap. Information ricochets in strange ways, and Bambaataa got the idea for his name from seeing the British movie *Zulu*, starring Michael Caine, directed by Si Endeback, a radical American who'd fled the McCarthy witch-hunts for Britain in the 1950s.

Bam's Projects were dominated by gangs, notably the Seven Crowns, whose rivals were the Black Spades. He joined in 1969, around the same time that he joined the Black Panthers. A peacemaker, Bam had friends in every camp. Bambaataa had the vision of hip-hop, specifically his Zulu Nation, being a family, an alternative to the gangs. Introduced to the progressive downtown scene by the artist "Fab Five" Freddy Braithwaite, as so many artists were, Bam spun his Zulu Nation set at the downtown Mudd club and was amazed at the response. Mixing together the prototypical German synthesizer group Kraftwerk with spaghetti Western music, Ennio Morricone's "The Good the Bad and the Ugly," he recorded "Planet Rock," a universal hip-hop anthem in 1982.

Aware rappers knew the significance of James Brown and liked to touch him, musically, for luck. When Bambaataa wanted to affirm Black solidarity, he linked up with James Brown for the single "Unity" in 1984.

The churning, burning machine of funk was kicked into gear in the 1960s by James Brown and rolled right across America, then the world, like a new religion. The sacrament is horn sections so polished they shine, riffing atop monster drum and bass teams. The dynamite funk of the "Godfather of Soul" asserted a vibrant energy on classic tracks like "Papa's Got A Brand New Bag" and "It's A Man's Man's World" or "Super Bad" and "Hot Pants." An elemental force, the power of Brown not only inspired, it galvanized. Like the big bands of the 1940s, James Brown's musicians moved in immaculate syncopation, and the interaction of the rhythm and horn sections, fronted by Brown's charismatic footwork, set off a chemical reaction that exploded at every show. As a child struggling in the streets of Georgia, Brown used to dance for small change. Grown into the master of funk, Brown's splits, leaps, and twirls were the crescendo of an array of rubber-limbed steps like the camel walk and the mashed potato.

As a mover, James had few peers until the advent of Michael Jackson's moonwalking. Jackson was a new breed of pop icon, with *Off The Wall* and *Thriller*. Jackson ruled the world in the mid-1980s, partly because he appeared to be a superior life form, with uncanny control of his voice and body. So slick were his moves that his slide seemed to glide, floating to Quincy Jones' compulsive production. Jackson became an international Prince Charming by being a good star—twinkling and untouchably high above. He penetrated pop like no other African American before him.

But Jackson couldn't have cut it without the funk. With its commitment to grooving on the one, a beat that bonds every listener, funk became a common denominator for a new nation of bands who could also claim Parliament's track "One Nation Under A Groove" as its national anthem. Like fine wine, every region had its funky variations. Unfortunately, some excellent vintages didn't travel well, like the go-go sound of Washington, D.C. bands like Chuck Brown and the Soul Searchers and Trouble Funk rumbled with an elemental thunder that the movie *Good To Go* tried to harness, but they remained local legends.

The loose, multicultural San Francisco scene nourished the effervescent Sly and the Family Stone, who represented an alternative society, beyond gender and color, in the late 1960s and early 1970's. The thumping thumb of their bass player Larry Graham "popped" the strings in an innovative style that later propelled his own funk band, Graham Central Station, and then kept Prince's funk burning. From Texas, the brothers, Ronnie, Charlie, and Robert Wilson's Gap Band sparked off new steps on the dance floor with off-beat gimmicks. The band's quirky personality comes across in the catchy synthesized bass and flip ad-libs of "Oops Upside Your Head" (based on P-Funk satellite the Brides of Funkenstein's "Disco To Go") and their stomping, "Burn Rubber On Me."

The squealing of gears and relentless New York City action intersects with wild animal noise in the heavy grooves of Kool and the Gang singles "Jungle Boogie" and "Funky Stuff." Their *Spirit of the Boogie* record references the spirit of the black chord, with titles like "Ancestral Ceremony" and "Caribbean Festival." "Early Kool and the Gang records are a mixture of jazzy sophistication and great R&B roots-rhythm music," commented Nile Rodger, the producer, guitarist, and cofounder of the disco era group, Chic.

Horn-heavy, Kool and the Gang were a command to dance, as Larry Blackmon's Cameo was an invitation to something more kinky. Coming from the seamier side of NYC, Larry Blackmon enjoyed exploiting his "Big Freak" potential (to quote the track by Miles Davis' wife, the silver-suited siren Betty Davis). An artistic descendant of the mascara-wearing rock'n'roller Little Richard, Blackmon upped the frisson of sexy songs like "She's Strange (But I Like It)" by flaunting bulging codpieces over spandex catsuits and exaggerated flat-top hairdos.

Lee Perry London 1984

Finley Quaye  London 1998

All that funky flamboyance was George Clinton's fault, flying in on his silver pyramid spaceship, the Mothership Connection, deploying the funk to fight the disco blahs he called the "Placebo Syndrome."

James Brown ran his organization like an army, even imposing fines if his artists failed to smile offstage. The flamboyant bassist Bootsy Collins was dismissed from the Famous Flames by the Godfather when Bootsy hallucinated that the neck of his bass turned into a snake onstage. "James Brown was street funk, and Funkadelic was do your own thing, and we did it. I mean, freaking for days...."[61] recalled Bootsy with satisfaction.

O'Funk that Clinton developed to people his parallel universe are iconic archetypes who satirize what Public Enemy would later call "Fear of a Black Planet." Unforgettably, Clinton renamed Washington, D.C.—home of the White House—"Chocolate City." The song has an exhilarating sense of the impending, inevitable victory of natural justice and builds to a crescendo with its rallying cry, "Gainin' on ya!"

"After 'Chocolate City,' I had to think of another situation that Blacks would just seem very weird in. Because Black is what's happening everywhere round the world, so it would be very stupid of us not to do like any other race and do what we got. Even though some of us would

London 1988
Jah Shaka

Sly and Robbie
London 1984

His red-and-silver-leather jumpsuits, garish platform shoes, and prowling, growling bass fit right in with the freewheeling P-Funk's exuberant anarchy of burly dudes in diapers or wedding dresses playing high-octane, lift-off funk.

Clinton wasn't alone in choosing the pyramid as a central rallying symbol. It embodies ancient Egyptian wisdom and, as architect I. M. Pei's glass pyramid in the Louvre demonstrates, eternal futurism. Relocating to a better planet somewhere between ancient Egypt and outer space is a potent metaphor for explorers like George Clinton, Sun Ra, Betty Davis, Earth, Wind, and Fire, and Labelle. Conditions on the home planet were not always conducive to feeling like a fully entitled citizen while America was unwilling to give up the funk, in the shape of real equal opportunity. The cast of characters like Sir Nose D'Void

like to be cool and sophisticated like White people; we're attracted to that, too, 'cause we've never had it. I realized that the majority of the world was just the opposite—they wanted a real serious Black man. I had to think of another situation that would look very cool and funny to put Blacks in, and we could get rid of a lot of live rhythms. "Nobody could ever conceive of a Black guy in a spaceship,"[62] laughed Clinton.

Like Clinton, Earth, Wind, and Fire incorporated a large pyramid structure into their live performances; it descended from above via an elaborate pulley system and was dressed in enough silver to supply solar energy to a small village. Before going onstage in their quintessential mid-1970s outfits, Earth, Wind, and Fire would hold hands in a circle and bow their heads in prayer—they were remarkably successful at

Notting Hill Carnival  London 1992

sneaking spirituality onto the disco floor. "Writing a song like "Serpentine Fire," which is about the kundalini yoga energy in the spine, nobody knows what I'm talking about," explained their leader Maurice White in 1979, "but a lot of kids go out and look it up and immediately it expands their consciousness."[63]

White named his production company Kalimba, after the southern African thumb piano that was used to conjure up ancestral spirits and also gave a unique texture to Earth, Wind, and Fire's music. The kalimba exerted a parallel pull over disco dancers who instinctively followed Earth, Wind, and Fire's exhortation to hold their heads up to the sky, because they were all shining stars.

**Bad Brains** London 1987

The spaceships of Clinton and White were virtual updates of Marcus Garvey's Black Star Liner, fuelled by high-grade music to ferry believers to a new, improved place. The imposing Sun Ra and his Arkestra, however, chose to visit Earth as emissaries and teachers from Saturn. "Space is the place, space is the place . . . When the world was in darkness and darkness was ignorance, along came Ra...." Audiences would sing along with Ra's vocalist, June Tyson.

An emperor in flowing, glittering robes, Sun Ra projected an otherwordly tranquil force that seemed to refract from the silver disc on his forehead—a crown that was later adopted by another space-age seer, Lee "Scratch" Perry. Magisterial at the keyboards, Ra led the Arkestra's brightly robed musicians through chants, blues, boogie-woogie, and lush symphonic jazz, and made them all flow like a river.

Although he was born Herman Blount in Alabama, Ra successfully erased much of his earthling identity, including his date of birth (early in the twentieth century). He got himself a new musical passport stamped "Saturn" and began filling notebooks with diagrams, theories, and facts like Leonardo da Vinci, and expounded obliquely on his metaphysical cosmology. He often spoke sonorously, looking away, but would suddenly flash a sly, cheeky smile. "They say that history repeats itself, but that's his story, not my story. My story is endless. It never repeats itself. Why should it? The sunset never repeats itself, nor the sunrise."[64]

Though seemingly eccentric, discipline was Ra's byword. "I really heard the intervals (and harmony) one night,"[65] explained longtime Arkestra saxophonist, John Gilmore, "and I said, my gosh, this man is more stretched out than [Thelonious] Monk, it's unbelievable." Ra ran a tight outfit in his musical collective in Philadelphia and affected his Germantown neighborhood with his dignity, his Egyptology, and his sense of cosmic possibilities.

Labelle joined Ra on the space shuttle in the disco era of the 1970s. Formed in their schooldays, Labelle had begun in church and in doo-wop harmonies, just like Clinton's Parliament; in fact, when Clinton had barbershops in the hood, he styled Nona Hendryx's hair. The original Patti Labelle and the Bluebelles were an archetypal female harmony trio in Detroit who, despite the scuffling inherent in dealing with small, independent labels, had national hits like "I Sold My Heart to the Junkman." Doo-wop prom queens, Labelle's members sewed their own first stage outfits, demure spaghetti-strap cocktail frocks with skirts as bouffant as their hair.

When their sound changed from doo-wop to rock'n'soul, Labelle retained their fundamentals—the spritualized histrionics of Patti LaBelle's vocals and Nona Hendryx's haughty hip. In her autobiography *Don't Block the Blessings*, Patti LaBelle credits designer Larry La Gaspi with creating the silver garb that "broke the three-girl-three gown mold wide open. Uniformity was a thing of the past. Individuality was Labelle's future. "[Larry] said his space suits did not mean we were from outer space or spaced out but that Labelle was futuristic, miles ahead of all the other girl groups."[66]

Though these Amazons were spectacularly

Eric B. & Rakim London 1987

Run DMC New York 1983

New York 1994 **RZA**

15²

De La Soul New York 1993

Horace Andy London 1985

Grandmaster Flash London 1987

Tricky New York 1995

Afrika Bambaataa London 1982

"Graffiti in London be fun"

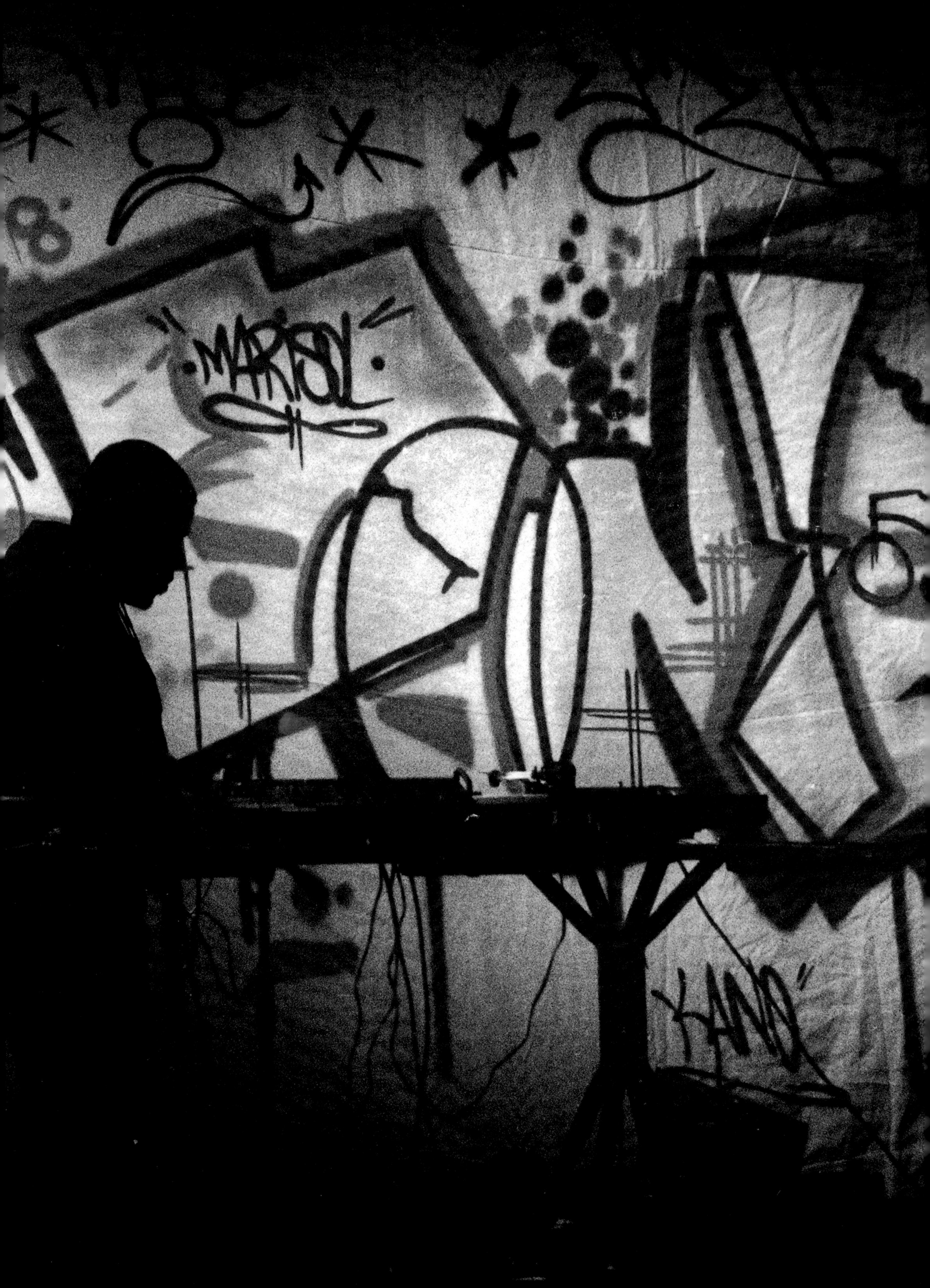
MARISOL
KANO

Previous page: Africa Bambaataa London 1982

shiny, their sound was earthy. It was rejuvenated by New Orleans's Allen Toussaint, whose swaggering production on "Lady Marmalade," with its sassy chorus "Voulez-vous couchez avec moi, ce soir" (Would you like to sleep with me tonight?), reeked of the heady perfume of a fantasy New Orleans bordello.

Instead of finding a shortcut to their best selves in a spaceship, some musical explorers puncture the thin membrane between cultures. They become messengers, transmitters who absorb and internalize different rhythms and feelings that even their own families might find alien.

With his easygoing, accessible grace, Ray Charles, "the Genius," made his blindness irrelevant as he blended Black R&B, soul, gospel, and White country into an all-American sound. "He was one of my gurus. He taught me how to arrange, how to voice horns and reeds," remembered Quincy Jones. "At a time when you were either in this camp or that camp, either a bebopper or a blues man or whatever, Ray was in every camp. 'It's all music, man' Ray would say. 'We can play it all.' And we did."[67]

In his trademark tuxedo and Ray-Ban™ shades, the welcoming roughness of Charles' voice and the allure of his arrangements cut through the barriers that divided America. He devised the instrumentation that became standard for R&B bands, refining the music down to piano, rhythm section, and a horn section of two trumpets and saxophones. Accustomed to call and response in church, Charles adapted that African tradition to pop, notably on his cheery 1961 track, "Hit The Road, Jack," in which he traded lines with Percy Mayfield.

All the rhythms of the islands that found their way into the Manhattan streets melted down in the music of August Darnell's Kid Creole and the Coconuts. With literate wit and perverse morality, the former English teacher spun stories over hot rhythms pilfered from across the Caribbean, spiced with New York funk. Their quintessentially "Nuyorican" (New York/Puerto Rican) music found more favor in Europe than at home. But Darnell made his point. "Creole is the combination of French and Blacks in New Orleans. I use it as a beautiful symbol of the amalgamation of different cultures, musically. Melodies have come to be associated with the white man's world of Rodgers and Hammerstein, Cole Porter, or Gershwin, which is as absurd as only associating rhythm with Africa."[68]

Darnell's specific mix of tropical and urban music was an amusing way to delve into some increasingly common shifts in cultural identity. On the same quest, numerous African diaspora artists have spent time absorbing Africa. The years that jazz pianist Randy Weston, lived in Morocco are audible in his music. Jazz-funk father Roy Ayers and avant-garde trumpeter Lester Bowie both lived with Fela's

Biz Markie London 1988

Spoonie G. London 1988

Kid Creole London 1984

156

# Georgeclinton
London 1985

London 1987

Kalakuta (Rascal's) Republic in Lagos, Nigeria. One of the founders of ska, the Jamaican guitarist Ernest Ranglin recorded with local musicians in Senegal and commented, "It was like finding a piece of myself that I had lost."

Finding new fusions to express the relationship between their continent and the rest of the world is a concern of many African musicians like Cheikh Lô and Senegalese rappers Positive Black Soul, who collaborated with MC Solaar, the leading stylist of French hip-hop. The Gambian griot Foday Musa Susa plays kora with such disparate artists as composer Philip Glass, the Kronos String Quartet and Herbie Hancock. "For these collaborations to work, you have to really listen to and understand the sort of music you'll be playing with," he stated.

Reggae's global messenger, Jamaican singer-songwriter Jimmy Cliff, toured extensively in Brazil and Africa and spread those feelings to his island culture. "It was a mission, though I wasn't conscious of it. It was to make a way, lay a foundation for this thing called reggae,"[69] said Cliff of a career that began in the ska days of the 1960s alongside the Wailers and Toots and the Maytals. The enterprising young singer scored a deal with Chinese-Jamaican producer Leslie Kong's Beverley's label with a specially written song "Dearest Beverley." Looking sharp in a slick suit, Cliff dropped Rastafarian references into his ska music, as in, "Lion say, I am king and I reign," which obliquely name checks Haile Selassie, King of Kings, aka the Conquering Lion of Judah. (Cliff later became Muslim.) He gathered fellow singers and welders Desmond Dekker and Bob Marley to join him at Beverley's and encouraged the seventeen-year-old Bob Marley to stop welding and stick to music after a spark damaged his eye. The fluting syncopation of singer Desmond Dekker, one of the original "rude boys" (street toughs) on tracks like "007" and "The Israelites" had a swaggering cool that helped define ska attitude.

Bob Marley chose to release his haunting 1960s Lee Perry production "Sun Is Shining" (also known as "To The Rescue") on his own Wail'N'Soul'M label, and loved it enough to record it for his 1977 album *Kaya*. "Not every song of Bob's should be sung," insisted Finley Quaye. But his insightful version of "Sun Is Shining" cuts to the bone. Touched by influences from folk to dub, Quaye makes ethereal, provocative music and takes pride in his Afro-Celt heritage. "I always think things should be revolutionary, to bring about change, and to do that you have to appreciate the past," he said. Brother Caleb is a well-known bass-player, and Tricky is a relative, but their way was paved by Quaye's grandfather Cab a Ghanaian musician who had one of the first Black orchestras in London, the Five Musical Dragons, in 1908. Taking inspiration where he finds it, Quaye's music reflects his credo: "I feel thoroughly Scottish, but the world is my home."

Trumpeter and world-jazz griot Don Cherry always invested his art in being a global citizen. He was an aficionado of instruments like Mali's hunter's guitar, the *dousn'gouni*. "I've been lucky to have met different masters from different countries who've shared their knowledge with me. I think it's important to know these cultures and really study them, otherwise it's just trying to play exotic music,"[70] he said.

Free spirit as Don Cherry was, he joked that he played his pocket trumpet because of its portability. Cherry was a Pied Piper who would enter a graffiti-studded subway carriage with an impromptu improvisation on the flute. Born in Oklahoma to a part-Choctaw family, Cherry was raised in Watts, where he sneaked in to watch Duke Ellington and Count Basie play at his father's jazz club.

His children became musicians; two became pop stars. His son Eagle Eye attributed the success of his bluesy country rock to Don's advice: Never be afraid to keep it simple. A pioneer female who fused melody and rap, Cherry's daughter Neneh (whose genetic father is Sierra Leonean drummer Amadu Jah), graduated from the prototypical woman punk band the Slits and free-jazz funkers Bristol's Rip Rig and Panic. She explores ideas of family in her music and was probably the first pregnant woman to get down on TV in form-fitting Lycra for her first single, "Buffalo Stance," in 1988. In her father's spirit, she collaborated with Youssou N'Dour on the haunting single "Seven Seconds," which became a global hit outside America in 1994.

London 1986

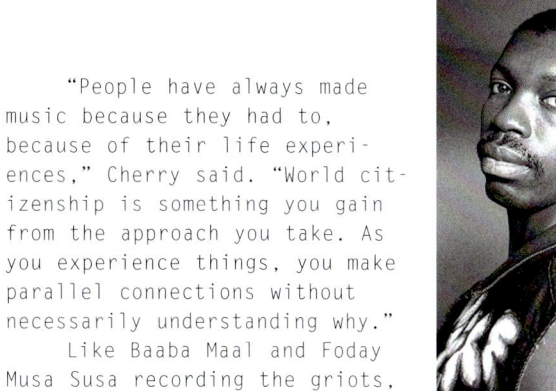

"People have always made music because they had to, because of their life experiences," Cherry said. "World citizenship is something you gain from the approach you take. As you experience things, you make parallel connections without necessarily understanding why."

Like Baaba Maal and Foday Musa Susa recording the griots, some artists commit themselves to ensuring the continued existence of jazz. In the forefront of archival preservation and education is New Orleans trumpeter and composer Wynton Marsalis and his Jazz at Lincoln Center program, which preserves classical jazz. The celebration of Duke Ellington's 1999 centennial had an educational emphasis; the band leader's scores were distributed among American schools and a competition for school big bands helped ensure the teaching of the big band tradition—at least among schools with sufficient funds to supply the instruments.

The pianist Ellis Marsalis encouraged his children Wynton, Delfeayo, and saxophonist Branford not only toward musical excellence, but also to immaculate presentation. The Marsalis clan always looks extra clean, as if defying the ramshackle image of the tragic geniuses of jazz; drunk, drugged, dishevelled icons like Bird. Their stance spells confidence and ease within the system; Wynton Marsalis became the official face of jazz in the White House, presenting artists like the ermine-voiced singer Dianne Reeves. Bussed to a hostile White school in Civil Rights-era Denver, Colorado, the young Reeves had participated in making music to teach racial awareness and seen it work.

The need to reassess and draw attention to the work of their predecessors also fires artists like the blind pianist Marcus Roberts, a protégé of Wynton Marsalis, who has reinterpreted the music of George Gershwin, James P. Johnson, and Father of Ragtime Scott Joplin, whose sheet music was the first to sell over a million copies in 1899. Often his rags sound stiff, as if performed by a player piano, but Roberts brings warmth and swing to Joplin's instrumentals. An associate of Roy Ayers and Ray Charles, vocalist Dee Dee Bridgewater succeeded in invoking Ella Fitzgerald on her 1990 tribute album, *Dear Ella*. Aspects of Ella's supple style have been adopted by singers like Al Jarreau, but as one of the few active vocalists with experience of big band singing, having worked with the Thad Jones/Mel Lewis Orchestra, Bridgewater can scat.

Adventurous spirits like Davis and Wilson ignore barriers or burst through them as rites of passage. The immaculate scatter and vocalizer Betty Carter once told a TV interviewer, "Be spontaneous—that's the beauty of jazz."[71]

That jazz tradition is associated with the maverick creativity of eternal explorers. Some musicians on a mission include John Coltrane, whose masterful saxophone and quest for spiritual enlightenment resulted in the transcendent *A Love Supreme*, an album that has come to define spirituality trapped on wax. Miles Davis continually explored with his trumpet. Speaking in a whisper, insulated by sunglasses, Miles turned his back on the frenzy of bebop and the audience, a lesson in cool.

New albums by these innovators were awaited like messages from the mountaintop. The jazz fathers' assertive titles like Davis' 1949 *Birth of the Cool* and Ornette Coleman's 1959 *Shape of Jazz To Come* clearly rang in the new for their particular moments. Their disciples have gone on to fire other artists, notably the alumni of Miles like Tony Williams, Herbie Hancock, and Wayne Shorter, who've spun off fusions like new planets: jazz-rock, Latin-jazz, techno-jazz, hip-hop jazz. The sophistication of jazz-funk was spread by numerous artists, including trumpeter Tom Browne; the smooth South African guitarist Jonathan Butler, and the West Coast band, the Crusaders, whose all-star cast included drummer Stix Hooper and saxophonist Wilton Felder, pianists Joe Sample and Larry Carlton. Collaborations with blues guitarist B.B. King and singers Bill Withers, Bobby Womack, and Randy Crawford plugged them into ever wider audiences during their thirty-five-year career.

Exquisite mood portraits like "Sketches of Spain" and "Kind of Blue," arranged by the whimsical, soft-spoken Canadian Gil Evans continued a progress of restless creativity. It took an abrupt turn when Miles married his second wife, the petite Betty Mabry, who commemorated their relationship in her track "He Was a Big Freak." An astro-gal long before Labelle, Mabry was an old flame of psychedelic funk-rock guitarist, Jimi Hendrix, whose gaudy velvet sexuality and orgasmic guitar gave the ageing Davis pause for thought. With a shock, Miles went electric in 1969 with his song "Bitches Brew" and jazz-rock emerged fully blown from his head, midwifed by Herbie Hancock, Wayne Shorter, Joe Zawinul, and drummer Tony Williams. When Miles started a new decade with "On The Corner," he relocated jazz to a contemporary urban address. His last recordings featured rappers on "Doo Bop," tying a beautiful bow in the black chord.

Born suburban, Miles dug the jolt of the streets—including the heroin that had become associated with jazzers like Charlie "Bird" Parker and dogged John Coltrane so badly that Miles fired him from the band, replacing him temporarily with the big-lung sound of "The Saxophone Colossus," Sonny Rollins. Tough love triggered a cleansing period for Coltrane, after which the saxophonist returned with a style called "sheets of sound." It was so different that whispers circulated about Coltrane selling his soul to the Devil for the sound—the same rumor that haunted blues-man Robert Johnson in the 1930s. Coltrane plunged into his most provocative "modal" music, approaching the scales from an unconventional angle that captured his increasing interest in Africa, Asia—and the Beyond.

"When we were playing with Miles,"[72] recalled Herbie Hancock with a smile, "if any of us ever made a mistake, he would rather we kept the mistake." Hancock furthered the experimental spirit in the early days of video. At a time when MTV was not playing Black artists Hancock recorded the rap-flavored "Rockit" in 1983 and promoted it with a droll futuristic video—minus an appearance by the actual artist. Its success spawned a school of electro-jazz-funk. "The first time I was into synthesizer music was with Herbie Hancock's "Headhunters," said guitarist and producer Nile Rodgers. "I was listening to all that lush orchestration, and then I looked at the back of the sleeve—not one string! I said, Whoahhh...."

A similar urge to explore moved the avant-garde into the decaying, gray, iron-clad canyons of post-industrial Manhattan in the early 1960s. They took advantage of the vast spaces and low—usually illegal—rents among the garment manufacturers and sweatshops south of Houston Street, an area that, decades later, would become fashionable Soho. There was a sense of liberty in this urban, wild frontier, though it was often chilly, shabby, and inconvenient. There were spaces like Ornette's loft on Broadway, which became a chic Calvin Klein store some decades later; Ali's Alley, the live/play space of drummer Rashied Ali; and Sam and Bea Rivers's Studio Rivbea. Playing of all sorts happened around-the-clock.

Amid this freewheeling semianarchy, Ornette honed harmolodics, a music in which each instrument pursues its own melody, ignoring the established structures of bars and chord changes that dictate when to shift gears. Many melodies become one as the musicians tune in deeply to one another. He's described the system as "removing the caste system from sound."

"There is a way of getting the sounds that you want at the place that you want them with the results that you want. They are available, it's just about how you go travelling that road to find them,"[73] Ornette explained. "Some rhythm sections eliminate the right to think and therefore you have to lock your ideas into their sound. Some people think this is a very good discipline for music, that you have a strict order of logic and you show how many variations this logic can mean to you emotionally. (But) that's all it's ever gonna do. It's not gonna free you from the cause of not needing."

Using plastic as well as more conventional instruments, Ornette staked a free jazz outpost. A school emerged around it, and prominent musicians, among whom were Anthony Braxton, who writes music in the form of diagrams, and saxophonist Sam Rivers. Rivers played with drummer Tony Williams who was a mature thirteen years old at the time. Rivers said, "[I] first got into the style I'm playing today as a player and a writer. I became interested in free playing from a classical point of view, abstraction, creating sound. That's different from Ornette's concept, which came out of the blues."

his interviews encouraged him to put down the pen and pick up the sax.

The horn is the closest instrument to the human voice, its vocabulary broadened by generations of players. The gutbucket, blues-based sound of a wailing horn section seasoned every 1960s and 1970s dance sound, from Clinton's P-funk to the great R&B hit factories like Atlantic, Stax, Al Green, and Willie Mitchell's Hi Records, the Philly Sound, and Motown. Horn giants infused pop with jazzy breadth like Aretha's beloved King Curtis and Junior Walker, whose tenor sax colored hits by the Temptations,

Kool and The Gang London 1982

New York 1994 Earth, Wind, and Fire

Williams grew up to play with Miles Davis and brought Rivers, his original mentor, into Davis' band. Rivers said, "Miles was still doing things that were...pretty straight....I kept stretching out and playing really long solos....Miles finally ended up playing free, but it was with static rhythm."[74]

Much as London junglist Goldie exults in the five generations of music he draws from, saxophonist/clarinetist David Murray relishes his position in a tradition. Before founding the World Saxophone Quartet with Arthur Blythe, Oliver Lake, and Hamiett Bluiett, Murray was interviewing his musical heroes for a thesis on jazz, which he planned to make into a book until

Marvin Gaye, Smokey Robinson, Stevie Wonder, and Tammi Terrell.

Trumpeters take the tradition in different directions. "Romantic Defiance," is the name Terence Blanchard, composer of movie soundtracks for director Spike Lee among others, gives to his lyrical tone, steeped in the feel of his beloved New Orleans brass bands. In its freewheeling communality, panethnic visual panache, and cultural depth, Lester Bowie's Arts Ensemble of Chicago recalled the Sun Ra Arkestra. He also brought whimsicality to the mainstream with the "avant-pop" ensemble Brass Fantasy, interpreting hits by Madonna, Marilyn Manson, and Michael Jackson.

"When I played with a band called New York

City in the mid-1970s, we supported the Jackson Five," recalled Nile Rodgers. "At soundcheck, they played "Dancing Machine." It was unbelievable. That's how magical the times were in those days. People were experimenting, coming up with new sounds, new grooves, new vibes.

Disco became a great cultural divide. Racing at the speed of the amyl nitrate poppers beloved in its birthplace, gay clubs, disco was reviled by rock'n'roll DJs who led a national Disco Sucks movement. It was equally loathed by "deep soul" artists who felt their brand of intense reality was being sidelined by party-down inanities. They felt disco's rigid four-on-the-floor beat was a fiendish, tyrannical rhythm that they were forced to play or die a commercial death. "Hmmm. Disco. I kind of lost my way there for a minute,"[75] laughed Curtis Mayfield.

"People called my band, Chic, a disco band; but we were the furthest thing from disco. The disco genius I look to, who revolutionized dance music, was Giorgio Moroder, an Italian who had a hit in Germany with a Black American woman, Donna Summer. Nile Rodgers explained. "To be played in these new places of worship called discotheques we played faster. The disco format was a really catchy melody and a good beat—from around 110 to 130 beats per minute. [It] just made people want to hit the dance floor. We just didn't know how powerful that format was."

Beyond the music, Chic's flip, bittersweet irony gave even such a seemingly superficial track as "Good Times" an edge: "You silly fool, you can't change your fate." Chic knew that the famous man in the moon eternally lifting a coke spoon to his nose who hung over the Studio 54 dance floor would sniff once too often and twirl out of control.

"Every big Chic song has a melancholy undercurrent. Though our band was making more money than you could imagine, we were in the midst of the biggest recession of my lifetime in America. We were saying, OK, we know AIDS exists, people are having problems with money, and we know the hedonistic lifestyle we're leading is causing it on some level, but do we stop?" Rodgers laughed, as if the prospect was unlikely.

Disco was important on more than a musical level to Rodgers. "For the first time in the history of Black music, we were not judged because we were Black. If you put that disco format on your record, you'd be on the radio just like the Bee Gee's."

The same issues of access to the industry confronted African American or Black British bands who resented always having to be "soulful"

Larry Blackmon (Cameo) London 1985

Gap Band Cannes 1983

Neneh Cherry
London 1982

Patti Labelle & Nona Hendryx
New York 1982

**Don Cherry** London 1982

**Sun Ra** London 1982

Ray Charles New York 1998

or "funky." Excited by British bands like the Beatles and Led Zeppelin, who had given a rock flash to the blues, punk rockers like the Sex Pistols and heavy metal rockers like Kiss and Aerosmith—who collaborated with Run DMC—demanded the right to be Black rockers.

Guitarist/producer Vernon Reid was a co-founder of the 1980s collective the Black Rock Coalition, with artists like writer and guitarist Greg Tate, drummer Marque Gilmore, and East Village funk-rockers Faith.

"What led up to the BRC was a growing sense of frustration. If you didn't play R&B or some kind of ethnic-identified music, you would not get signed. I called people together and said, 'Is it just me, or is some racism going on?'" recalled Reid. "Then it became, What are we going to do to get it changed? We started to do concerts. It was pretty exciting."

Reid gives respect to Black rockers who played it before the genre had a name. In England, photographer Dennis Morris formed the raucous Basement Five in the early 1980s with filmmaker Don Letts, who doubled as a DJ—turning punks on to reggae at the original Roxy club in Covent Garden. Inspired by London's punky reggae party, Washington, D.C.'s Bad Brains mixed up hardcore thrash with punk and reggae.

In such interchanges, cultural miscegenation feeds Baaba Maal's tree of music and helps it grow in new directions. As Vernon Reid explained, "The whole idea with rock'n'roll is very tribal and racial. That's really changing a lot now. Ice Cube looks like Marilyn Manson."

Continuously adapting, the black chord is an infinite progression. Musing in its richness, Vernon Reid said, "[t]here's also the song of love, and the song with no real purpose in mind that's what dub is all about, feeling the moment you're in, living in that vibration. That's the power of Santeria, of voodoo, and the Pentecostal Church. Those vibes are inexpressible."

Sonny Rollins New York 1998

Miles Davis London 1985

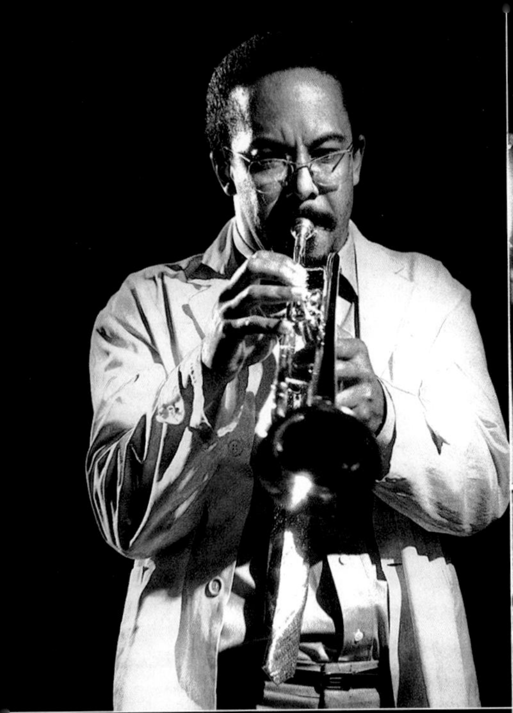
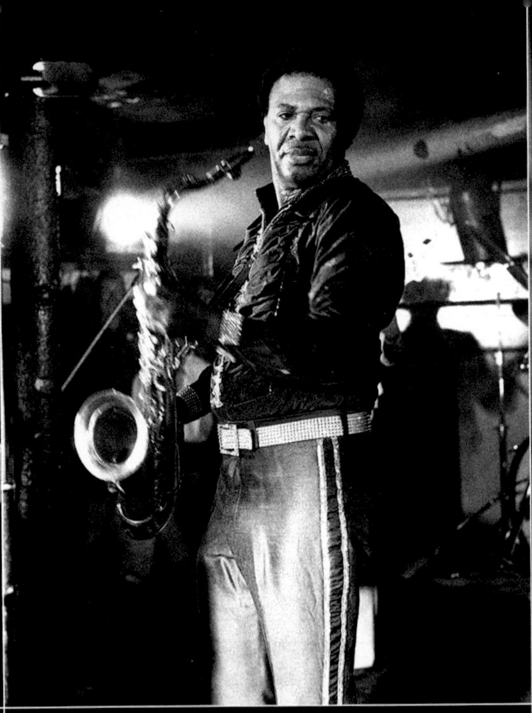
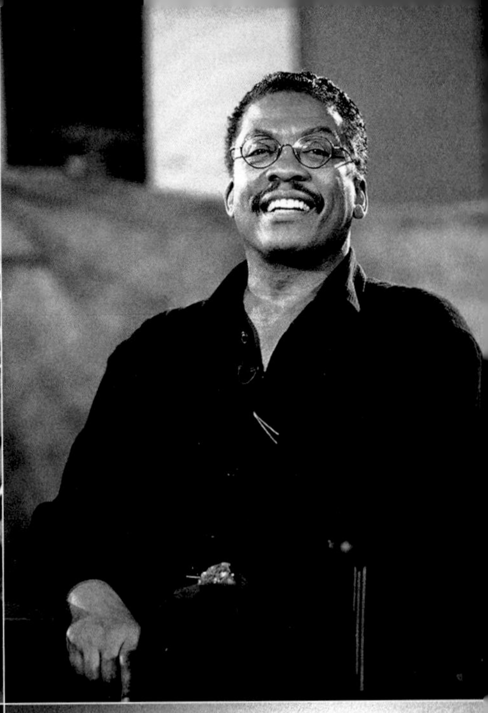
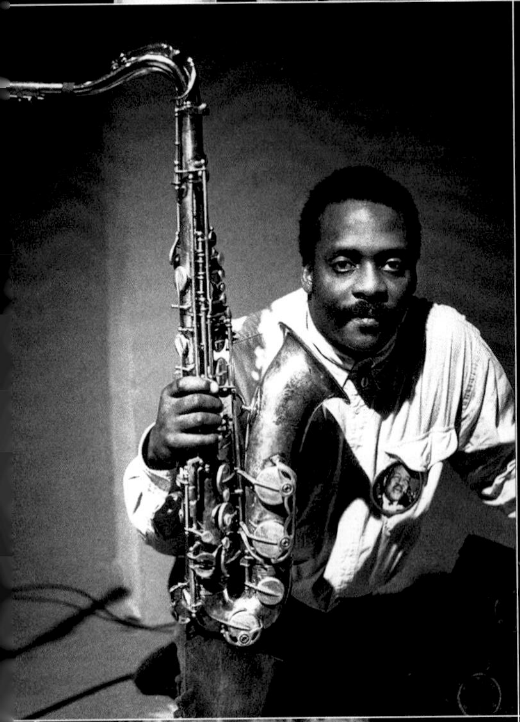
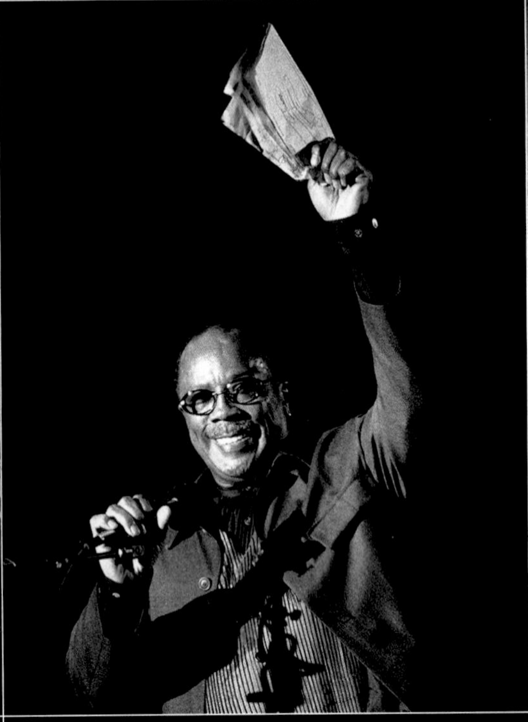
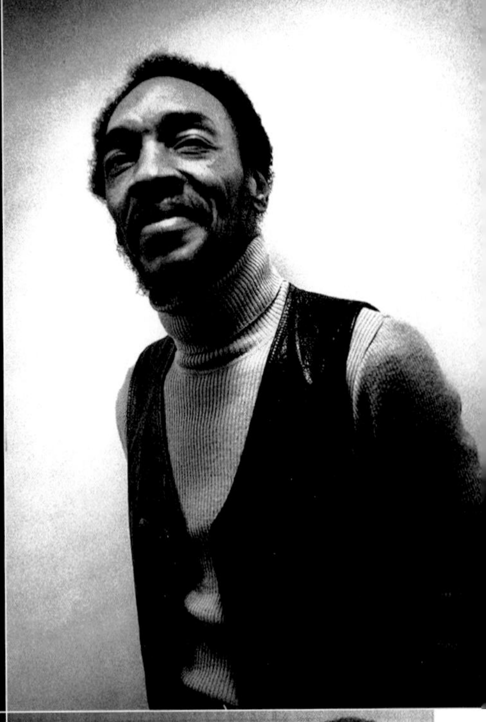
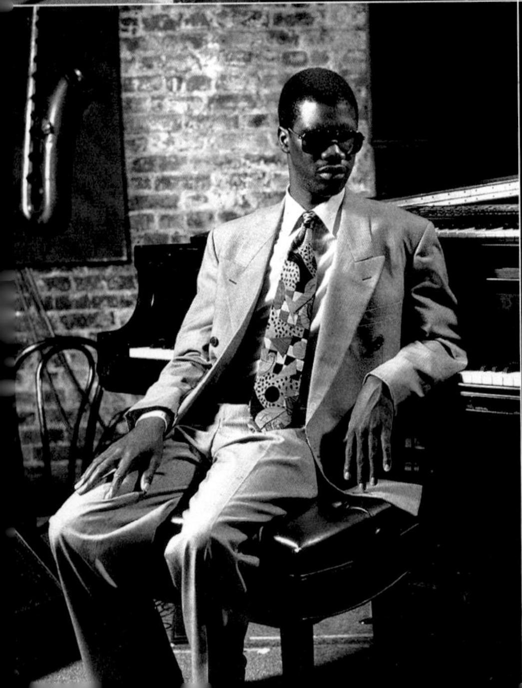
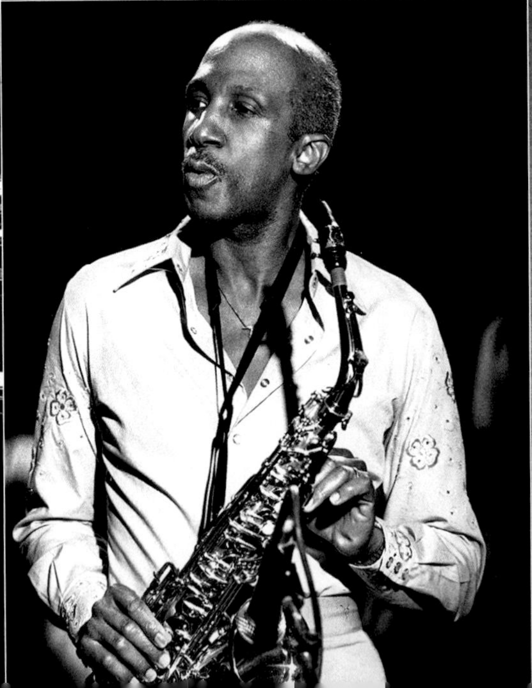
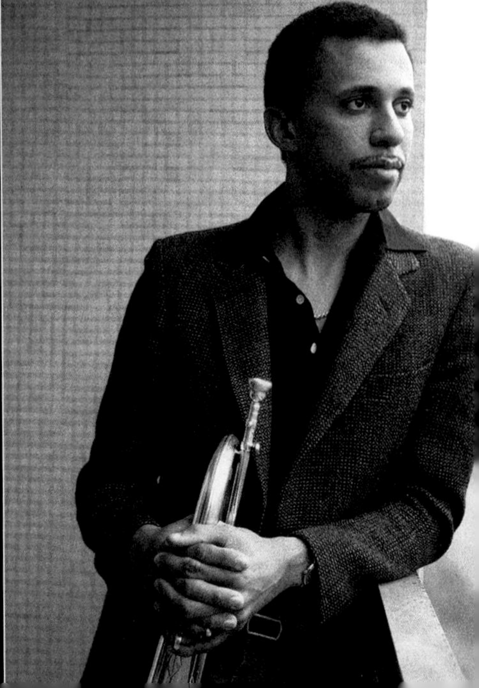

Opposite top row: Lester Bowie, Bracknell, England 1982  Jr. Walker, London 1980  Herbie Hancock, New York 1998  Opposite middle row: David Murray, New York 1995  Quincy Jones, New York 1998  Sam Rivers, London 1980  Opposite bottom row: Marcus Roberts, Washington D.C. 1994  Wilton Felder, London 1984  Tom Browne, London 1995

This page top row: Jazzy Jeff & Fresh Prince, London 1986  Roy Ayers, New York 1998  This page second row: Jimmy Cliff, New York 1993  Desmond Dekker, London 1985
This page third row: Dianne Reeves, New York 1998  Al Jarreau, London 1986  This page fourth row: Coxsone Dodd, New York 1992  Basement 5, London 1981

Shinehead

London 1989

Vernon Reid

New York 1999

London 1987 Augustus Pablo

Nile Rodgers (Chic) New York 1998

# INDEX

*References to photographs are printed in italics.*

Aaliyah, 62
Abyssinians, the, 37, *49*
Ade, King Sunny, 55, *56*
Adu, Sade, 78, *79*
Afrobeat, 127
Alemany, Jésus, 23
Anderson, Vicki, 106
Andy, Horace, 142, *153*
Angelou, Maya, 98
Anikulapo-Kuti, Fela, 97, 127, *96*
apartheid, 98
Arnaz, Desi, 23
Arrested Development, 114, *116*
Artist, the, 60-61, *63*
Aswad, 122, 140, *132*
Ayers, Roy, 156, *169*
B., Anthony, 123, *132*
B., Eric, 142, 144, *151*
Bad Brains, 165, *150*
Badu, Erykah, 32, 36, 108, *49*
Bambaataa, Afrika, 142, 144-145, *153*, *155*
Banton, Buju, 83, *84*
Basement Five, 165, *169*
Be, Prince, 114
Beenie Man, 83, *84*
Belafonte, Harry, 98
Beverly, Frankie, 62, *72*
Big Youth, 122, 142, *124*
Biggie Smalls.
  *See Notorious B. I. G.*
Black Rock Coalition, 139, 165
Black Uhuru, 122, *132*
Blackmon, Larry, 145, *162*
Blakey, Art, 26, *33*
Blanchard, Terence, 161
Bland, Bobby 'Blue,' 27, *28*
blaxploitation, 114
Blige, Mary J., 78, 88-89, *77*
Blind Boys of Alabama, *37*
Blount, Herman. *See Ra, Sun*
blues, 27, 32, 60, 67
Boukman Eksperians, 123, *133-134*
Bowie, Lester, 156, *168*
Brandy, 67, *70*
Bridgewater, Dee Dee, 159
Brown, Chuck, 145, *158*
Brown, Dennis, 122, *99*
Brown, Foxy, 88

Brown, James, 102, 106, 107, 140, 144, 145, 148 *109-111*
Brown, Jocelyn, 78, *76*
Browne, Tom, 159, *168*
Burning Spear.
  *See Spear, Burning*
Burundi, 18
Byrd, Bobby, 106, *112*
Cachao, 26, 28
calypso, 39, 40
Cape, Roy, 39, *50*
Carmichael, Stokeley.
  *See Toure, Kwame.*
Carnival, 23, 26, 123
Castro, Fidel, 23
censorship, 107
Charles, Prince, 74, *65*
Charles, Ray, 156, *165*
Cherry, Don, 158, *164*
Cherry, Eagle Eye, 158
Cherry, Neneh, 107, 142, 144, 158, *163*
Chic, 162
Chimurenga music, 127
Civil Rights Movement, 97, 106
Cliff, Jimmy, 158, *169*
Clinton, George, 148, *157*
club music, 78
Cole, Natalie, 56, *76*
Coleman, Ornette, 9, 115, 139, 159, 160-161
Collins, Albert, 32, *43*
Collins, Bootsy, 55, 148, 160
Collins, Lyn, 106
Coltrane, John, 159, 160
Cooke, Sam, 62, 64
Cortez, Jayne, 27, 97, 115, 118, *32*
Cray, Robert, 32, *46-47*
Cruz, Celia, 26, *28*
Cuba, 23, 26
Cu-bop, 26, 98
Culture Club, 78, 140
Dammers, Jerry, 118
dance, 15, 23, 145
D'Arby, Terence Trent, 62, *64*
Darnell, August, 156.
  *See also Kid Creole and the Coconuts*
Davis, Miles, 15, 26, 123, 159, 160, *166*
Dawn, P. M.,114, *119*
De La Soul, 144, *153*
Dekker, Desmond, 158, *169*
Denton, Sandy, 88

Desvarieux, Jacob, 123
Dioubate, Oumou, 56
disco, 148, 162
Dodd, Coxsone, 78, 123, 127, *169*
Domino, Fats, 26, *35*
Downing, Will, 60, *61*
drums, 18, 23
dub, 139, 140
Dunbar, Sly, 40, 140, *148*
Earth, Wind, and Fire, 139, 148, 150, *161*
Edison, Harry 'Sweets,' 26, *32*
Edmonds, Kenneth 'Babyface,' 74, *73*
Ellington, Duke, 26
Elliott, Missy, 9, 27, 83, 89, 107, *88*
Ellis, Alton, 78, 83, *82*
Exodus Steel Band, 18, *22*
Felder, Wilton, 159, *168*
Fitzgerald, Ella, 159
Flash, Grandmaster, 142, *153*
Flavor Flav, 97, 107
Four Tops, 60, *57*
Franklin, Aretha, 64, 74, 102, *102*
Franklin, Kirk, 27, 36, 62, *39*
Fresh Prince.
  *See Smith, Will*
Fresh, Doug E., 15, 142, *19*
Fugees, 67, 108, 123, *103*
Funi, Bi, 56-57
funk, 145
Gaillard, Slim, 15, 139, *143*
Gaines, Will, 14, *14*
gangs, 88, 107
Gap Band, the, 145, *162*
Garvey, Marcus, 39, 150
gay clubs, 75, 78
Gaye, Marvin, 62, 106, *66*
Gee, Spoonie, 144, *156*
Gillespie, Dizzy, 98
Gilmore, John, 150
Glover, Savion, 15, *17*
Golden Arrow, 26, *32*
Goldie, 41, *51*
Gordy, Berry, 106
gospel, 27, 37, 56, 64, 67
Graham, Larry, 145, *160*
Grant, Eddy, 40, *43*
Green, Al, 60, *54*
Griffiths, Marcia, 36, *48*
griots, 15-16, 27, 39, 55, 56, 106-107, 158

Guthrie, Gwen, 78, *76*
Haiti, 23, 123, *31*
Hammond, Beres, 83, *85*
Hancock, Herbie, 160, *168*
Hayes, Isaac, 114, *5*
Hendrix, Jimi, 160
Hendryx, Nona, 150, *163*
Hill, Lauryn, 67, *103*
  (also see Fugees)
hip-hop, 74, 107-108, 139, 140, 142, 144-145
Holloway, Brenda, 75, *80*
Holt, John, 83
Hooker, John Lee, 27, *42*
Houston, Cissy, 67
Houston, Whitney, 67, *67*
Hyman, Phyllis, 75, *76*
Ibrahim, Abdullah, 26, *34*
Ice T, 107, *117*
Isaacs, Gregory, 83, *85*
Jackson, Michael, 9, 62, 97, 145, *100-101*
Jackson, Millie, 88, *77*
Jamaica, 36, 37, 56, 83, 118, 122-123, 142
James, Cheryl, 88
James, Rick, 74, *73*
Jarreau, Al, 159, *169*
jazz, 15, 26, 32, 98, 115, 139, 159, 161
Jazzbo, Prince, 108, *118*
Jazzy Jeff, 144, *169*
Jean, Wyclef, 26, 144, *103*
  (also see Fugees)
Johnson, Linton Kwesi, 97, 108-114, 115, 118, 123, 140, *120*
Johnson, Robert, 55
Jolly Boys, *29*
Jones, Grace, 140, *141*
Jones, Quincy, 23, 97, 98, 145, 156, *168*
kalimba, 150
Keita, Salif, 16, 18, 36, 55-56, *21*
Kelly, R., 60, 61, *71*
Khan, Chaka, 78, *77*
Kid Creole and the Coconuts, 156, *156*
King, B. B., 27, 32, *44*
King, Ben E., 60, *56*
King, Evelyn 'Champagne,' 78, *76*
King, Martin Luther, Jr., 97, 102
Kool and the Gang, 145, *161*
kora, 16, 27
KRS-1, 114, *118*
Kuti, Fela. *See*

174

Anikulapo-Kuti, Fela
L L Cool J, 75, *86*
Labelle, Patti, 150, *38, 163*
Lady Saw, 88, *69*
Ladysmith Black Mambazo, 15, *16*
Last Poets, 115, *116*
*L'Authenticité*, 10
L'il Kim, 88, 106
Lincoln, Abbey, 98, 102
Lion, Roaring, 39, 40, *50*
Luciano, 123, *132*
Maal, Baaba, 9, 16, 18, 27, *20*
Mabry, Betty, 159
McFerrin, Bobby, 15, *16*
McGregor, Freddie, 83, *84*
Madame Chic-Choc. See Sangare, Oumou
Mahal, Taj, 32, *43*
Makeba, Miriam, 9, 56, 98, *103*
Mali, 56
Mandela, Nelson, 118, 122
Mapfumo, Thomas, 127
Markie, Biz, 144, *156*
Marley, Bob, 9, 36, 37, 56, 83, 97, 106, 122, 123, 127, 158, *126-127*
Marley, Rita, 36, *48*
Marsalis, Wynton, 159, *45*
Masekela, Hugh, 98, *103*
Massive Attack, 140, 142
Mayfield, Curtis, 67, 74, 106, 114, 162, *72*
Mbuli, Mzwakhe, 122
Method Man, 74-75, *91*
Miller, Jacob, 122, *130*
Mitchell, Willie, 60, *62*
Monica, 9, 27, 55, 67, 78, *11*
Motown, 106
Mowatt, Judy, 36, *48*
Murray, David, 161, *168*
Mutabaruka, *120*
N'Dour, Youssou, 16, 18, 36, 123, 158, *58*
Neville Brothers, the, 23
Neville, Aaron, 62, *56*
New Jack Swing, 83
New Orleans, 23, 26, *30*
New York, 26
Nigeria, 55
Northern Soul movement, 75
Notorious B.I.G., 83, 88, *89*
Odetta, 97, *103*
Olatunji, Babatunde, 18

Oney, *8*
Onura, Oku, 118, *120*
Pablo, Augustus, 139, *172*
Papa Wemba. See Wemba, Papa
Parker, Maceo, 106, *113*
Perkins, Pinetop, 26, *41*
Perry, Lee 'Scratch,' 139, 140, *146*
Pine, Courtney, 15, *32*
Pipecock Jackson. See Perry, Lee 'Scratch'
poetry, 118
praise song, 55
Prince Jazzbo. See Jazzbo, Prince
Prince. See Artist, the
Public Enemy, 97, 107, *117*
Puma, 122
punk rock, 123
Quaye, Finley, 10, 158, *147*
Ra, Sun, 150, *161*. See also Sun Ra and his Arkestra
Rakim, 142, 144, *151*
Ranglin, Ernest, 158
Ranks, Shabba, 83, 142, *85*
rap, 74, 75, 83, 107, 108, 114, 139, 142, 144-145
Rastafarian, 36, 122, 123, 139
Reagan, Bernice Johnson, 97
Reeves, Dianne, 159, *169*
reggae, 36, 40, 83, 108, 122-123, 139, 140
Reid, L.A., 74
Reid, Vernon, 139, 165, *171*
religion, 23, 26-27
Rhodesia, 127
Riley, Teddy, 74, *73*
Ritchie, Lionel, 62, *69*
Rivers, Sam, 161, *168*
Roach, Max, 98
Roaring Lion. See Lion, Roaring
Roberts, Marcus, 159, *168*
Robinson, Smokey, 60
Rodgers, Nile, 75, 145, 160, 162, *173*
Rodriquez, Virginia, 23, *28*
Rollins, Sonny, *166*
roots music, 32
Run DMC, 142, *151*
RZA, 60, 144, *152*
Sade. See Adu, Sade
Salt N' Pepa, 88, *87*
Sangare, Oumou, 56
*sapeurs*, 10
Scott-Heron, Gil, 97, 118, *120*
Seko, Mobutu Sese, *10*

Shabalala, Joseph, 15
Shaka, Jah, 140, *148*
Shakespeare, Robbie, 140, *148*
Shakur, Tupac, 107
Shante, Roxanne, 108, *118*
Sharpeville Massacre, 98
shebeens, 140
Shinehead, 142, *170*
Simone, Nina, 97, 106, *103*
Size, Roni, 40, *29*
ska, 37, 78, 123, 127, 158
Skatalites, 127
slavery, 6, 9, 10, 18, 36, 60
Sly and the Family Stone, 145
Smalls, Biggie, 107
Smith, Bessie, 55, 60
Smith, Carrie, 27, *36*
Smith, James Todd. See L L Cool J
Smith, Michael, 9, 118, 122, *121*
Smith, Will, 144, *169*
South Africa, 15, 98, 118
Spear, Burning, 36, 37, *29*
Spector, Phil, 75
Spector, Ronnie, 75, *77*
Stalin, Black, 39, *50*
steel pan, 18, 39
Steel Pulse, 123, *131*
Sugar Hill Gang, 144
Sun Ra and his Arkestra, 150. See also Ra, Sun
Sus, 123
Susa, Foday Musa, 16, *27*
Taj Mahal. See Mahal, Taj
tanbour, 23
techno music, 40
Temptations, the, 106, *114*
Terrell, Tammi, 62, 106
"The Door of No Return," 9
Toots and the Maytals, 37, 56, *56*
Tosh, Peter, 122, *128-129*
Toure, Kwame, 56, 98
Touré, Sekou, 55-56
Toussaint, Allen, 156
tribute songs, 56
Tricky, 140, 142, *153*
Trinidad, 18, 39
Trouble Funk, 145, *159*
Turner, Ike, 75
Turner, Tina, 75, *77*
Ulmer, James 'Blood,' 32, *43*
U-Roy, 142, *125*
Vance Ensemble, 27, *36*

Vandross, Luther, 74, *73*
Vietnam War, 106
voodoo, 23, 123
Wailer, Bunny, 37, *50*
Wailers, the, 37, 122, 123
Walker, Junior, 161, *168*
Ward, Clara, 64
Warwick, Dionne, 67, 74, *81*
Wash, Martha, 75, *57*
wassoullou, 56
Watson, Johnny 'Guitar,' 83, *90*
Weather Girls, the, 75, *57*
Wells, Junior, 32, *41*
Wemba, Papa, *10*
Weston, Randy, 156
White, Barry, 60, 62, 88, 89, *59*
White, Maurice, 150
Wild Magnolias, 26, *29*
Williams, Tony, 161
Wilson, Cassandra, 32, *40*
Winans, the, 27
Withers, Bill, 74, *73*
Womack, Bobby, 62, 64, 114, *68*
Wonder, Stevie, 106, *115*
Wu Tang Clan, 60, 74, 144
Zaire, 10
zouk, 123
Zulu Nation, 145

# ENDNOTES

*All persons not cited have been interviewed specifically for the making of this book.*

## Introduction
1. Papa Wemba, CD notes for Paul Bradshaw, *Emotion*, Real World Records, 1995.

## Roots & Culture
2. Miles Davis with Quincy Troupe, *Miles Davis: The Autobiography* (Touchstone/Simon & Schuster).
3. Foday Musa Susa, *Jali Kunda, Griots of West Africa and Beyond* (Ellipsis Arts).
4. *Jali Kunda*.
5. *Jali Kunda*.
6. Paolo Hewitt, "On the Block With Quincy Jones," *Straight No Chaser*, Spring 1990.
7. Vivien Goldman, "Wyclef Jean Knows the Score," *Rhythm Music*, Oct./Nov. 1997.
8. "Wyclef Jean Knows the Score."
9. *Miles Davis*.
10. Ben Sidran, *Talking Jazz* (Da Capo).
11. *Jali Kunda*.
12. B. B. King with David Ritz, *Blues all Around Me* (Hodder & Stoughton).
13. Vivien Goldman, *Soul Rebel*, *Natural Mystic* (Eel Pie and St. Martins Press, 1981).
14. Vivien Goldman, "The Spear Guide to Higher Stepping," *NME*, Feb. 1981.

## Heart and Soul
15. Vivien Goldman, "Don't Leave Home Without your F.U.N.K." *Sounds*, June 24, 1978.
16. Smokey Robinson with David Ritz, *Inside My Life* (McGraw Hill).
17. Allan Lewis and Gavin Petrie, eds., *Black Music* (Hamlyn).
18. Vivien Goldman, "Soul Searching," *Melody Maker*, Oct. 9, 1976.
19. Vivien Goldman, "That's All, Y'All," *Sounds*, March 27, 1976.
20. Barney Hoskyns, "The Soul Stirrer," *Mojo*, Jan. 1995.
21. Vivien Goldman, "Resurrection of Mayfield's Soul," *Daily Telegraph*, Jan. 25, 1997.
22. Epic Records press release, 1986.
23. Vivien Goldman and Janette Beckman, interview in *Jammin' Video Magazine*, 1991.
24. Esther Iverem, "Over the Edge," *Essence*, July 1996.
25. Vivien Goldman, "Johnny Be Baaad," *Mojo*, May 1995.
26. "Johnny Be Baaad."
27. Interview with Vivien Goldman on the MTV special "Ain't Nothing but a She Thing," Good Karma Productions, 1995.
28. "Ain't Nothing but a She Thing."
29. Vivien Goldman, "Women Have Got to Work Harder than Men or They End Up Sleeping with Everyone and God Knows I Don't Want to Do That," *Rolling Stone*, Nov. 13, 1997.
30. "Women Have Got to Work Harder."

## Revolution
31. Maya Angelou, *The Heart of a Woman* (Bantam).
32. Interview with Vivien Goldman on the program "African Ambassador," Spellbound Pictures, BBC Arena, 1985.
33. "African Ambassador."
34. "African Ambassador."
35. "African Ambassador."
36. "African Ambassador."
37. *The Heart of a Woman*.
38. Tom Terrell, "The King's Queens: James Brown's Original Funky Divas," *Seconds*, no. 47.
39. "The King's Queens."
40. Robert Katz (producer), "The '70s," VH1, 1997.
41. "The '70s."
42. "Ressurection of Mayfield's Soul."
43. Vivien Goldman, "Black in the USA," Spin, Oct. 1992.
44. Sally B. Donnelly, "A Voice from the Hood Takes his Message to the World," *Emerge*, Sept. 1992.
45. Mimi Valdes, "Things Done Changed," *Vibe*, Oct. 1995.
46. "Ressurection of Mayfield's Soul."
47. Bill Adler, Rap: *Portraits and Lyrics of a Generation of Black Rockers* (St. Martin's Press, 1991).
48. Vivien Goldman, "Harmolodic Harlem," *Village Voice*, Sept. 3, 1996.
49. Tom Terell, "Full Revolution," XXL, Issue 3, Vol. 2, no. 1.
50. Vivien Goldman, "Movement of Jah People," *Sounds*, May 29, 1977.
51. C. C. Smith, "Talking to Youssou," *Africa Beat*, Summer 1987.
52. Larry Birnbaum, "Voodoo on the Jukebox," *Pulse*, Nov. 1992.
53. Vivien Goldman, "The Lion of Zimbabwe," *New Musical Express*, Jan. 5, 1985.
54. Vivien Goldman, "The Rascal Republic Takes on the World," *New Musical Express*, Oct. 18, 1980.
55. "The Rascal Republic Takes on the World."

## Explorers
56. Vivien Goldman, "On Feeling Human," *New Musical Express*, July 10, 1982.
57. Vivien Goldman, "Lee Perry Has Found God and His Name is Pipecock Jackson," *Melody Maker*, July 1997.
58. Vivien Goldman, "Freedom into Form," *Melody Maker*, Dec. 23, 1978.
58. Vivien Goldman, "A Big Big Sound System Splashdown," *New Musical Express*, Feb. 21, 1981.
59. Gravegiggaz EPK (press release).
60. "Wyclef Jean Knows the Score."
61. Vivien Goldman, "Don't Leave Home without Your F.U.N.K.," *Sounds*, June 24, 1978.
62. Vivien Goldman, "Free Your Mind Your Accountant Will Follow," *Melody Maker*, Nov. 25, 1978.
63. Vivien Goldman, "Maurice White's Banc of Hope," *Melody Maker*, March 10, 1979.
64. Robert Mugge (producer/director), A *Joyful Noise* (documentary film), 1980.
65. *A Joyful Noise*.
66. Patti Labelle with Laura B. Randolph, *Don't Block the Blessings* (Bolevard Book).
67. David Ritz and Julie Stover, eds., CD booklet for *Fifty Years of Genius and Soul*, Rhino Records, 1997.
68. Vivien Goldman, "He No Pop I," *New Musical Express*, July 4, 1981.
69. Vivien Goldman, "A Pioneer Returns," *Melody Maker*, Feb. 3, 1979.
70. Kathryn Willgress, "World Jazz Griot," *Straight No Chaser*, Winter 1990.
71. TV interview on "Sunday Morning," CBS, October 1998.
72. "On Feeling Human."
73. Robert Palmer, *Downbeat*, 1975.
74. "Ressurection of Mayfield's Soul."
75. "Ressurection of Mayfield's Soul."